HOMELAND SECURITY
OPERATIONAL ANALYSIS CENTER

The Role of Intellectual Property in U.S. Homeland Security

GEOFFREY MCGOVERN, MARIA MCCOLLESTER, DOUGLAS C. LIGOR,
SHENG TAO LI, DOUGLAS YEUNG, LAURA KUPE

Published in 2019

Preface

This research report is part of a two-stage study for the U.S. Department of Homeland Security (DHS) Science and Technology Directorate (S&T). S&T asked the Homeland Security Operational Analysis Center (HSOAC) to explore the connection between intellectual property (IP) functions and DHS and component mission areas to document how and when IP supports, enhances, and otherwise provides essential elements of mission success. Additionally, S&T asked HSOAC to explore situations in which a lack of a robust IP support system has revealed weaknesses or inefficiencies in DHS and component operations.

This research was a preliminary investigation into the current baseline level of IP support at the department and the components. This baseline is intended to guide DHS's planning efforts in a new area of IP functionality: Invention Secrecy Act of 1951 (Pub. L. 82-256, 1952) reviews. However, S&T first requires an understanding of what IP functions are already provided and currently needed and what level of effort is needed to maintain a robust IP program that supports the full range of mission functions within DHS's purview. The findings of this report should be of interest to policymakers involved in legal affairs, resource planning, innovation and invention management, research and development, and intellectual property at the department and component levels.

This research was sponsored by the DHS Office of General Counsel, Technology Programs Law Division, and conducted within the Acquisition and Development Program of the HSOAC federally funded research and development center (FFRDC).

About the Homeland Security Operational Analysis Center

The Homeland Security Act of 2002 (Section 305 of Public Law 107-296, as codified at 6 U.S.C. § 185), authorizes the Secretary of Homeland Security, acting through the Under Secretary for Science and Technology, to establish one or more FFRDCs to provide independent analysis of homeland security issues. The RAND Corporation operates HSOAC as an FFRDC for DHS under contract HSHQDC-16-D-00007.

The HSOAC FFRDC provides the government with independent and objective analyses and advice in core areas important to the department in support of policy development, decisionmaking, alternative approaches, and new ideas on issues of significance. The HSOAC FFRDC also works with and supports other federal, state, local, tribal, and public- and private-sector organizations that make up the homeland security enterprise. The HSOAC FFRDC's research is undertaken by mutual consent with DHS and is organized as a set of discrete tasks. This report presents the results of research and analysis conducted under Procurement Instrument Identifier (PIID) 70RSAT18FR0000132, Protect DHS IP.

The results presented in this report do not necessarily reflect official DHS opinion or policy.

For more information on HSOAC, see www.rand.org/hsoac. For more information on this publication, see www.rand.org/t/RR3039.

Contents

Figures and Table

Figures

Table

Summary

This research report is part of a two-stage study for the U.S. Department of Homeland Security (DHS) Science and Technology Directorate (S&T) on the department's approach to management of intellectual property (IP). S&T asked the Homeland Security Operational Analysis Center (HSOAC) to explore the connection between IP functions and missions of the department and its component agencies to document how and when IP supports, enhances, and otherwise provides essential elements of mission success. S&T also asked HSOAC to explore situations in which shortcomings in the IP support system have revealed weaknesses or inefficiencies in DHS and component operational activities and to then make appropriate recommendations to address the shortcomings. This report represents the results of a preliminary investigation into that current baseline level of IP support at DHS and its components.

DHS currently takes a federated approach to IP management. IP management is centralized at the secretary level, with each of the subordinate agencies and offices retaining the authority to create and manage its own IP programs. The secretary further delegates responsibility for IP management to three offices within the department: the Under Secretary of Homeland Security for Science and Technology, the Office of the General Counsel, and the chief procurement officer. These offices are the keepers of DHS IP policy and collectively oversee the infrastructure for coordinating the work of IP staff at the department and component levels.

Our team of HSOAC researchers met with attorney staff at DHS headquarters and in the components. Although some of these staff members are trained IP attorneys, we learned that others are general attorneys who have taken on the responsibility of being points of contact for IP matters within their respective components. Additionally, we conducted semistructured interviews and document and policy reviews, and we reached out to program-level points of contact to collect opinions on IP needs, awareness, and emerging areas of concern.

We understand that DHS is already engaged in the regular production, acquisition, and deployment of IP assets. Our research into the existing IP activities at DHS revealed that various dimensions of IP are currently implemented in every component of the agency. Despite the universality of IP-related operations, the degree of integration and level of professional IP support available varies significantly across the enterprise. In all the cases we examined, IP is currently managed as a secondary support function rather than as a direct element of operational risk management. By *secondary support function*, we mean that IP is not routinely viewed as an asset that advances mission success but rather as an ancillary activity like accounting or purchasing is. Because IP activities are not as visible to the public (as, for example, a flood insurance program, security screening at airports, or patrolling the coastal waterways), IP has not been directly incorporated into mission planning and strategic positioning.

We believe that this arrangement does not serve the department's long-term interests because it underutilizes IP as a strategic asset that can reveal new strengths and weakness in department programming, can help actively manage mission risks, and can help position the department as an innovative agency that both creates and deploys IP and technology more broadly in service to the United States. As a result, we recommend that DHS consider alternative approaches to funding and organizing IP functions to better include IP management as an element more closely connected to organizational success. We provide some alternatives that the department might wish to consider; however, we note that, as the department begins planning Invention Secrecy Act of 1951 (Pub. L. 82-256, 1952) reviews and as increasing reliance on technology drives IP closer to the forefront of decisionmaking, the department should reevaluate both funding and organization to best meet the needs of programs, components, and the department overall.

Our interviews, literature reviews, and case study examinations confirmed that, although DHS is an organization founded to protect national security and U.S. IP, it is underutilizing an asset that can be deployed in that fight. The department can use the IP it creates or acquires to protect the United States, its people, and critical infrastructure. We believe that new policies should be considered to develop the right structure, level of support, and integration of IP functions into the DHS decisionmaking process.

Acknowledgments

Lavanya Ratnam, assistant general counsel for intellectual property, U.S. Department of Homeland Security (DHS), sponsored this work. Numerous attorneys and subject-matter experts across DHS and its components provided their input throughout the report. To them, we express sincere gratitude and appreciation.

At RAND, Richard Silberglitt and Michelle Grise provided invaluable commentary and recommendations. Isaac R. Porche III, Lisa Bernard, Gordon T. Lee, and Patrice Lester were instrumental in bringing this report to completion. We thank everyone for their help. Any factual errors or misjudgments remain the authors' responsibility, alone.

Abbreviations

CBP	U.S. Customs and Border Protection
CISA	Cybersecurity and Infrastructure Security Agency
CRADA	cooperative research and development agreement
CTPAT	Customs Trade Partnership Against Terrorism
CWMD	Countering Weapons of Mass Destruction Office
DHS	U.S. Department of Homeland Security
DNS	Domain Name System
DoD	U.S. Department of Defense
DOJ	U.S. Department of Justice
ERO	Enforcement and Removal Operations
FAR	Federal Acquisition Regulation
FEMA	Federal Emergency Management Agency
FFRDC	federally funded research and development center
FLETC	Federal Law Enforcement Training Center
GRaDER	Graduated Rad/Nuc Detector Evaluation and Reporting
HSI	Homeland Security Investigations

HSOAC	Homeland Security Operational Analysis Center
ICANN	Internet Corporation for Assigned Names and Numbers
ICE	U.S. Immigration and Customs Enforcement
ICRC	International Committee of the Red Cross
INS	U.S. Immigration and Naturalization Service
IP	intellectual property
ISA	Invention Secrecy Act of 1951
MMP	Missing Migrant Program
MPEP	*Manual of Patent Examining Procedure*
NASA	National Aeronautics and Space Administration
NPPD	National Protection and Programs Directorate
OEM	original equipment manufacturer
OGC	Office of the General Counsel
OGC/IP	Office of the General Counsel Intellectual Property Group
OPLA	Office of the Principal Legal Advisor
POC	point of contact
QHSR	Quadrennial Homeland Security Review
R&D	research and development
S&T	Science and Technology Directorate
TPLD	Technology Programs Law Division
TSA	Transportation Security Administration
USCG	U.S. Coast Guard

USCIS   U.S. Citizenship and Immigration Services

USPTO   U.S. Patent and Trademark Office

WMD   weapon of mass destruction

CHAPTER ONE

Introduction

This research report is the result of the first stage of a two-stage study for the U.S. Department of Homeland Security (DHS) Science and Technology Directorate (S&T). S&T is responsible for managing intellectual property (IP) initiatives for the department. The Office of the General Counsel's (OGC's) Intellectual Property Group (OGC/IP) is responsible for the development and management of an IP program on behalf of S&T.

S&T asked the Homeland Security Operational Analysis Center (HSOAC) to explore the connection between IP functions and DHS and component mission areas. Our objective has been to assess and document how IP functions can support, enhance, and otherwise provide essential elements to mission success. S&T also asked HSOAC to explore situations in which a lack of a robust IP support system has revealed weaknesses or inefficiencies in DHS and component operational activities.

This research was a preliminary investigation into the current baseline level of IP support at DHS and its components. This baseline should help inform decisions about appropriate resourcing for the IP support at DHS and the components and is intended to inform DHS planning efforts in a new area of IP functionality: Invention Secrecy Act of 1951 (ISA) (Pub. L. 82-256, 1952) reviews. S&T needs to have a comprehensive understanding of the IP functions that DHS currently provides. Furthermore, DHS leadership will need to understand the resources required to deploy a robust IP program with the capacity to support the full range of mission functions within DHS's purview.

In the second stage of this study, our team of HSOAC researchers explored the department's specific needs relative to process, workflow, staffing, and approach to implementation of ISA requirements. As a result, although we briefly discuss ISA matters in Chapter Two, the remainder of this report is dedicated exclusively to non-ISA IP matters. Our goal is to offer insights in support of S&T's programmatic responsibilities related to technology and IP policies. The research will help identify the evolving needs of legal staff responsible for planning, managing, and executing technology policy at DHS to comply with federal statutes, regulations, and internal guidelines. In so doing, it will help S&T continue to improve the way it manages the IP program and portfolio throughout the department.

We begin this chapter by recounting a recent set of cybersecurity events that the U.S. federal government faced. These events, which took place in early 2019, highlight the importance of having robust IP capabilities at DHS and support the need for HSOAC's research efforts. In this chapter, we also discuss the applied methodology in conducting this research, documentation of findings, and delivery of our recommendations.

A Framing Case

On January 22, 2019, the director of the Cybersecurity and Infrastructure Security Agency (CISA), a component of DHS, issued an all-government emergency directive about federal entities' vulnerabilities to cyberattack (CISA, 2019). Through CISA, the department was actively monitoring persistent tampering with the Domain Name System (DNS), including domain names of executive branch agencies. The DNS underlies the internet architecture for the .gov domains and such subdomains as that for the Federal Emergency Management Agency (FEMA). According to the emergency directive, "attackers have redirected and intercepted web and mail traffic and could do so for other networked services." These infrastructure-hijacking campaigns amounted to "significant and immediate risks to agency information and information systems," requiring CISA to mandate that all government agencies take immediate action. The emergency directive ordered every federal agency to determine whether it was a target of these attacks, take active measures to reset passwords, strengthen security posture with multifactor-authentication processes, and monitor systems for continued malicious activity.

The emergency directive deployed active measures to respond to the imminent threats facing government agencies; however, it did not leverage all protective assets at DHS's disposal.[1] DNS infractions, such as those perpetrated against the U.S. government, can be addressed through legal and regulatory means managed by the nonprofit Internet Corporation for Assigned Names and Numbers (ICANN). ICANN manages the root domain name registries and is the go-to resource when law enforcement, government agencies, and victims of domain name hacking require swift action to eliminate DNS tampering. ICANN's efforts, however, require DHS to initiate a protest in the DNS dispute resolution process. DHS did not do this in January, nor did the emergency directive instruct it to do so.

The omission of ICANN DNS measures was the result of a DHS resource being overlooked: the IP corps, attorneys who have specific training and experience in IP-related matters. These attorneys have expertise in internet protocols, technology, and operations and an appreciation for the IP dimensions of the DNS. We believe that these skill sets and personnel resources can increase the effectiveness of DHS responses to threats, such as the DNS tampering in January 2019. If directly integrated into department and component operations, IP resources can help DHS exercise its mission capabilities more efficiently, more effectively, and at reduced cost to the taxpayer.

This report documents DHS's needs and capabilities for a robust IP program in pursuit of that goal.

---

[1] Complicating matters was that DHS was one of the agencies subject to the monthlong partial government shutdown. See Sands, 2019.

Our Approach and Methodology

Motivation and Approach

DHS has five core mission areas—preventing terrorism and enhancing security, securing and managing borders, enforcing and administering immigration laws, safeguarding and securing cyberspace, and ensuring resilience to disasters—all of which have integral functions that rely on IP. This includes encouraging, protecting, and licensing innovations and inventions; preserving, protecting, and enforcing copyright and trademarks that the department uses to market and identify key programs; and conducting ISA reviews. S&T was given the responsibility of managing IP initiatives for the department. In addition to providing legal guidance, OGC/IP is responsible for developing and managing an IP program on behalf of S&T.

OGC/IP, in collaboration with S&T, provides mission support that ensures that the department is fulfilling its responsibility to safeguard the American people and the homeland. A robust IP program offers a strategic asset in accomplishing the DHS missions. Alternatively, weak IP actions can inject unexpected and damaging disruptions that increase mission risk. This research was designed to help S&T and OGC/IP evaluate department-wide IP needs and offer recommendations for how to continue building a robust IP program. As part of that focus, the project aimed to (1) clarify and communicate the importance of the IP program to mission fulfillment; (2) identify representative gaps, conflicts, and areas in which the existing program is not meeting DHS needs; (3) explore DHS components' reliance on IP functions; and (4) estimate the required resources for development of a more robust IP program.

Research Methodology

We conducted a scan of the types of IP issues that DHS regularly encounters, investigated the management authorities and organizational structures for conducting IP-related work, and performed a gap analysis to determine points of weakness in the program. As a core aspect of our research, we spoke with IP staff at the department and component levels to learn about the work being performed. We spoke with representative attorneys from each of the nine components, either in person or by phone, and conducted follow-up correspondence where necessary. Most of the components have sole attorneys who handle IP issues, but we also held some group conversations when multiple staff were involved in IP affairs. We sought to understand the ongoing mission activities that these staff currently support and to identify the components' program-level needs. From the project sponsor, we obtained the list of contacts (which was developed by each component in response to a request from the Secretary for points of contact for ISA reviews), who briefed the interview participants about the study's background and goals. We also developed a semistructured interview protocol that was vetted by the RAND Corporation's Institutional Review Board. The semistructured protocol allowed us to elicit the participants' expert opinions in a way that provided both consistency (based on a set of core questions and topic areas that all participants were asked to answer) and flexibility, whereby interviews could help narrow down topic areas based on the unique needs of each component. We found this to be a particularly useful dimension of the protocol, given the significant differences between the mission areas served by components, such as the U.S. Secret Service and the Transportation Security Administration (TSA).

With the first-round interviews complete, we conducted a comparative analysis across the components. We sought to identify the similarities and differences in how each component engaged with IP assets. We culled the interviews, mission areas, and public web presence to understand the similarities in activities and needs, the dimensions of unique reliance on IP, and both the number and level of specially trained IP staff within each of the components. Our investigation sought to determine whether all components dealt with core IP areas (e.g., invention disclosures, patenting, procurement support), whether the components had unique requirements (e.g., litigation management, active licensing or commercialization, international partnership stewardship), and whether they retained IP staff with specialized training to satisfy these requirements. DHS currently faces the challenge of structuring a department-wide IP program in accordance with S&T's overarching responsibilities while supporting the variation in component resourcing, demand for IP activity, and unique histories and cultures. We conducted a thorough investigation into these lines of effort to ensure that we did not suggest a "one-size-fits-all" approach at the department level. By increasing our understanding of the direct connection between IP functions and mission risk categories, we hoped to make informed recommendations for DHS leadership.

We then created a matrix of impacts that could arise from the effective management or mismanagement of IP assets. These potential benefits and risks are the result of a thought experiment that paired the categories of IP assets (and the functions of IP staff attorneys) with their roles in mission success and failure. We created the matrix as a tool to communicate these risks to DHS leadership and offer a visual justification for implementing a more holistic IP management approach. The matrix considers the harms and benefits to DHS and its components along five dimensions of risk: reputational, operational, credibility, innovation, and financial and litigation risks. When IP is well managed, the risk of harm is reduced, and benefits can accrue to the department. When IP is mismanaged or ignored, the risk of harm is exacerbated, and mission effectiveness can be subsequently eroded. The matrix, then, should serve as a heuristic to guide decisionmaking and identify associated risks from IP assets.

In this report, we have also included two additional lines of effort to assist the reader in developing a more holistic appreciation of the discussed issues. The first is an overview of IP concepts as a "primer" for audiences that might not be familiar with the role of law in protecting IP resources and how IP assets intersect with DHS mission areas. We have distilled this material in Chapter Two as an on-ramp for readers who are new to the topic. Additionally, we have provided a background overview for planning ISA implementation at DHS. The ISA directs the secretary of any defense agency to request a secrecy order barring publication and release of information related to a patent application filed with the U.S Patent and Trademark Office (USPTO) when release of the information would threaten national security.[2] DHS intends to begin implementation of ISA requirements in the near future. S&T will coordinate this activity, although it is likely to rely on

---

[2]   Section 85 of Executive Order 13286 (Bush, 2003) designated DHS a defense agency.

support from component subject-matter experts. Given that implementation of the act was one impetus for this study, we reviewed the act and the basic structure and processes at the USPTO and explored ways that implementation could affect components' IP activities.

Structure of the Report

Following this introduction, Chapter Two offers a brief primer on IP for readers who are new to the topic. In addition to providing a summary of core concepts, we focus on defining the types of IP that are relevant to DHS mission needs. (Readers who possess familiarity with IP can skip this section.) Chapter Three introduces DHS, its history, and its core mission areas. DHS's history—derived from many component parts with varied relationships to technology, law enforcement, and threat assessment—presents a challenge to designing and deploying an IP program for such a diverse mix of stakeholders. By focusing on mission areas, the nexus between threats and success, and the benefits of comprehensive IP integration, we present how a robust program model will traverse the unique histories and cultures of DHS elements. In Chapter Four, we present a notional framework for ways in which IP support can manage different aspects of program risk while supporting overarching mission goals. Additionally, we highlight stories of situations in which IP functions that are essential to supporting mission success in the department and its components are being overlooked. Our purpose is to inform DHS leadership on how IP skills and contributions can bolster mission success. Finally, in Chapter Five, we review our findings and provide policy recommendations for the department to consider during IP capacity-planning and implementation of ISA reviews.

In the appendix, we provide component-by-component reports on the state of IP support and critical needs at each of the DHS divisions. We found common themes within this analysis, which has formed a baseline set of common IP needs—particularly in supporting the components' contracting and procurement functions—and the need to tailor IP programming to the special characteristics of each component. We found that components that engage in more research and analysis activities require more patent and licensing support. Contrastingly, components that have more public-facing programs require support by trademark registries, monitoring, and enforcement to protect program trust against erosion because of enterprising third parties seeking to profit by misappropriating DHS trademarks. Still other programs require sophisticated IP attorney support to defend the department from patent-infringement lawsuits and allegations of IP impropriety. These component reports are the products of the research and interviews we conducted, and they reflect the on-the-ground experiences of DHS IP staff.

CHAPTER TWO

What Is Intellectual Property?

In this chapter, we provide background information on IP, IP law, and national security concerns related to that area of law. The first portion of this chapter is intended to serve as a primer on IP and related legal underpinnings: copyright law, patent law, and trademark law. The chapter then briefly discusses IP in connection with federal acquisition and procurement activities and concludes with a discussion of the ISA. The chapter will help familiarize lay readers with topics with which they might be unfamiliar in the context of DHS's far-reaching roles and responsibilities.

Intellectual Property

IP consists of intangible creations of the human mind, such as inventions, art, and written works, that are entitled to legal protection. IP laws grant creators the right to exclude others from reproducing their creations. This right enables creators to profit by monopolizing the creation or by charging others a licensing fee. The purpose of granting such rights is to encourage further innovation and creativity. Indeed, the U.S. Constitution specifically authorizes Congress power to grant "Authors and Inventors the exclusive Right to their respective Writings and Discoveries" in order "[t]o promote the Progress of Science and useful Arts" (Art. I) Congress has exercised this power to create three general categories of IP protection: (1) copyright law, which protects creative works; (2) patent law, which protects inventions; and (3) trademark law, which protects market identification, such as brands and logos. Additionally, federal procurement law protects contractors' technical data and computer software as those contractors' IP. All these areas of IP and IP law are important to DHS, although not every component experiences all these issues or experiences them to the same degree of intensity. More detail on specific component IP needs are presented in the appendix.

Copyright Law

Federal copyright law was established in a 1976 act for the general revision of copyright law (Title 17 of the U.S. Code), commonly known as the Copyright Act (Pub. L. 94-553). That law defines *copyright-protected material* as "original works of authorship fixed in any tangible medium" (§ 102). These works can include such products as literature, music and sound recordings, graphics, films, and architecture.

The definitive component for copyright is creative expression. A database of facts and figures, for instance, lacks the requisite creativity (*Feist Publ'ns, Inc. v. Rural Tel. Serv. Co.*, 1991).[1] Moreover, "[i]n no case does copyright protection . . . extend to any idea, procedure, process . . . or discovery, regardless of the form in which it is described, explained, or embodied" (Pub. L. 94-553, § 102). Nor are functional aspects of a work protectable. If the creative expressions within a work are not separable from nonprotected facts, ideas, or functional aspects, none of that work can be copyrighted.[2] This principle plays an important role in determining the applicability of these regulations to com-

---

[1]   The creativity threshold is low: Federal courts have clarified that arrangement of information, such as cookbook recipes or automobile values, is sufficiently creative to warrant copyright protection. See *Publ'ns. Int'l, Ltd. v. Meredith Corp.*, 1996; *CCC Info Servs. v. MacLean Hunter Mkt. Reports, Incl.*, 1994.

[2]   As the First Circuit explained, when

> the topic necessarily requires, if not only one form of expression, at best only a limited number, to permit copyrighting would mean that a party or parties, by copyrighting a mere handful of forms, could exhaust all possibilities of future use of the substance. (*Morrissey v. P&G*, 1967)

puter software, in which the lines between functional and expressive code are often blurred.[3]

Copyright protection attaches once the work becomes "fixed in any tangible medium," which could be in writing, an audiovisual recording, or even temporarily saved in a computer's random-access memory (*MAI Sys. Corp. v. Peak Computer, Inc.*, 1993). The copyright holder does not need to register the material with the U.S. Copyright Office to enjoy protection. Before 1978, an author needed to provide notice of copyright (usually denoted by "©" along with authorship and date) or risked forfeiting copyright protection. The 1976 Copyright Act permitted an author to cure an omission of notice, and the Berne Convention Implementation Act of 1988 (Pub. L. 100-568) eliminated the notice requirement altogether for all works created after 1989.

The copyright holder enjoys exclusive rights to reproduce, display, distribute, and perform the work and to prepare derivative works (Pub. L. 94-553, § 106). This protection lasts until 70 years after the author's death and enables the owner to sue any violator in federal court for copyright infringement. An important limitation to copyright protection is that "the fair use of a copyrighted work . . . is not an infringement of copyright" (Pub. L. 94-553, § 107). *Fair use* refers to using a portion of copyrighted material for a valuable social purpose. Four factors determine whether use of copyrighted material is considered fair use:

- the purpose and character of the use: whether the copied portion creates social value or new meaning independent of the original work
- the nature of the original work: more flexibility for copying factual than fictional work
- substantiality of the portion copied: the amount and importance of the copied portion in relation to the overall work

---

[3] See, e.g., *Oracle Am., Inc. v. Google Inc.*, 2014, *cert. denied*, 2015 (finding "header" codes and "structure, sequence, and organization" of functional code packages to be copyright protected).

- market effects: whether copying deprives the copyright holder of potential income.

Common examples of fair use include parody and displaying small snippets of a work. For instance, the novel *The Wind Done Gone* (Randall, 2001) was determined not to be copyright infringement of *Gone with the Wind* (Mitchell, 1936), despite reusing several iconic characters, because it was parodic (*SunTrust Bank v. Houghton Mifflin Co.,* 2001).

The Copyright Act explicitly excludes works of the federal government from copyright protection (Pub. L. 94-553, § 101). Therefore, court opinions, congressional records, and executive agency documents fall in the public domain and may be reproduced freely. But the federal government must still respect the copyright protection of private authors. Indeed, Congress expressly provided that a copyright may be "infringed by the United States" and permits a copyright holder to file suit against the government in the U.S. Court of Federal Claims (28 U.S.C. 1498[b]).

DHS faces copyright issues in unique ways. As part of the government, DHS cannot copyright the material it creates (per 17 U.S.C. 105). Government publications are part of the public domain. But the government must take care to observe others' copyrights. This includes use of others' photos, graphics, text, and recordings (both audio and visual). Use of these materials can raise IP concerns in contracting and procurement activities.

Patent Law

An inventor of "any new and useful process, machine, manufacture, or composition of matter, or any new and useful improvement thereof" may apply to obtain a patent from the USPTO (35 U.S.C. 101).[4] Pat-

---

[4]   The Patent Act further protects design patents, which are not utilitarian but ornamental. See 35 U.S.C. 171. And a separate statutory scheme protects asexually produced plant patents. See the Plant Patent Act of 1930 (Pub. L. 71-245) and Plant Variety Protection Act of 1970 (Pub. L. 91-577).

ents can be obtained on almost any useful product or process.[5] "But excluded from such patent protection are laws of nature, natural phenomena, and abstract ideas" (*Diamond v. Diehr*, 1981, p. 185).[6] Prior to 2013, only the inventor (the first person to conceive of an invention and reduce it to practice) may obtain a patent.[7] The United States switched to a first-to-file system in 2013, whereby a patent can be granted to the first person to file an application, even if the filer was not the first to invent the creation (Pub. L. 112-29, 2011).

Public Law 96-517, commonly known as the Bayh–Dole Act of 1980, sets forth patent policy for federal agencies that fund research and development (R&D) activities. The recipient of federal R&D funds is considered the inventor of any patentable technology and generally retains ownership of any invention developed with federal funding.[8] The inventor, however, must disclose the invention to the federal agency, file appropriate patent applications, and attempt to commercialize the invention. If the inventor fails to take these steps, the federal government can exercise the "march-in" right and take control of the invention.[9] Finally, the inventor must provide the federal government with a nontransferable and irrevocable license to use the invention.

The process for obtaining a patent from the USPTO is called *prosecution*. The patent application must describe the invention to enable a practitioner in the relevant field to make use of it (35 U.S.C. 112[a]). Although the applicant need not disclose all relevant information, the application may not omit any integral parts (*Christianson v. Colt Industries Operating Corp.*, 1989, *cert. denied*, 1989 [nondisclosure of specifi-

---

[5] See *Diamond v. Chakrabarty*, 1980 (a genetically engineered life-form was patentable); *State St. Bank & Trust Co. v. Signature Fin. Grp.*, 1998, *cert. denied*, 1999 (a business method can qualify as patentable subject matter).

[6] See also *Bilski v. Kappos*, 2010 (financial hedging was an unpatentable abstract idea).

[7] See 2011 America Invents Act (Pub. L. 112-29), which grants an inventor who publicly discloses an invention a one-year exclusive period to file an application.

[8] Under the portion of Bayh–Dole Act codified at 35 U.S.C. 202(a)(ii), a federal agency can determine that "exceptional circumstances" exist such that a modification in the patent right disposition provided under the act would better promote its objectives.

[9] The federal government can also take control for other reasons, such as health and safety concerns.

cations regarding component interchangeability did not invalidate an M-16 rifle patent because "the disclosure need generally be no greater than" the claimed invention]).[10] During prosecution, a USPTO patent examiner reviews the application to determine whether it is directed at patentable subject matter and whether it contains an adequate description for how others will be able to use it; the examiner also reviews utilization reports.

Before granting a patent, the examiner must also determine that the invention is both novel and nonobvious. Novelty requires that the invention be previously unknown to the public.[11] Importantly, prior knowledge that was classified, kept as an industrial secret, or otherwise publicly inaccessible does not negate novelty.[12] Nonobviousness requires that the invention provide a meaningful advance beyond prior knowledge. The difference between the invention and prior knowledge must not be so small that it would have been obvious for a skilled practitioner in the relevant field to make the requisite leap (see *KSR Int'l Co. v. Teleflex Inc.*, 2007). The nonobviousness inquiry recognizes that "inventions in most, if not all, instances rely upon building blocks long since uncovered, and . . . discoveries almost of necessity will be a combination of what, in some sense, is already known" (*KSR*, 2007). Thus, an invention that combines preexisting and well-known components can still be nonobvious, particularly if the invention (1) receives commercial success, (2) satisfies a long-felt but unresolved need, or (3) solves a problem that had been met with persistent failure (*Truswal Sys. Corp. v. Hydro-Air Eng'g, Inc.*, 1987, p. 1212).

---

[10] Patents filed prior to 2013 must also have disclosed the inventor's subjective belief that the application showed the best method in practicing the invention (*Christianson*, 1989, p. 1301). The America Invents Act eliminated the best-mode requirement (also called the best-method requirement).

[11] At one time, federal law considered an invention novel if it was unknown and unused *within the United States*. The America Invents Act changed this standard to worldwide novelty for applications filed after 2013.

[12] Certain exceptions apply. For instance, the Atomic Energy Act specifically states that, unlike what is the case for other types of secret information, "knowledge or use . . . under secrecy within the atomic energy program of the United States" "shall be a bar to the patenting of such invention or discovery" (Pub. L. 83-703, 1954, § 155).

If the USPTO grants a patent, the inventor has the exclusive right to make and use the invention for a set period, usually 20 years from the date of application. Other people or organizations seeking to make or sell the invention during this period must obtain permission from the inventor—a license. Patent infringement occurs not only if someone makes or sells an item identical to the invention but also if someone makes or sells a substantially equivalent item.[13]

The patent holder can claim infringement in federal court and can obtain an injunction to stop the infringement (see *eBay Inc. v. MercExchange, L.L.C.*, 2006, pp. 393–394), receive compensatory damages ("the court shall award the claimant damages adequate to compensate for the infringement, but in no event less than a reasonably royalty" [35 U.S.C. 284]), and enjoy other remedies. Punitive damages can be assessed only where infringement is willful (35 U.S.C. 283). The federal government has specifically waived sovereign immunity and permits patent holders to file infringement lawsuits against the United States in the Court of Federal Claims (28 U.S.C. 1498).[14] There is no option for jury trial in patent-infringement suits against the government, and available remedies are more limited: The patent holder can recover compensatory damages but cannot enjoin the federal government from using the invention.

DHS faces patent issues in several ways. From a technology innovation perspective, the department is engaged in the creation and exploration of new technologies through its laboratories and testing centers. New inventions, techniques, procedures, and knowledge are generated as part of these organizations' activities and can be protected through patents. This can happen when the government is the property owner (when government employees and funds created the new technology) or when the government acquires rights in new technologies through a funding recipient or collaborator. Different rules regard-

---

[13] Under the doctrine of equivalents, infringement can occur if the item in question performed substantially the same function in substantially the same way to achieve substantially the same result. Another formulation of this test states that insubstantial differences do not preclude infringement (*Warner-Jenkinson Co. v. Hilton Davis Chem. Co.*, 1997, pp. 39–40).

[14] Unlike in district courts, where infringement actions against private actors can be filed, jury trials are not available in the Court of Federal Claims.

ing governmental ownership rights are involved, hence requiring specialized knowledge in patent law and procurement expertise.

The department also needs to be aware of the way it can run afoul of others' patents. Patent-infringement cases—when the government uses a patented technology without explicit permission and payment of a probable licensing fee—present a litigation and financial risk to the department. Such a lawsuit is not likely to result in an injunction against use of the technology, but such suits can damage relationships with contractors, mar public opinion of the department, and erode progress toward mission success.

Trademark Law

Trademarks are the third main area of federal IP law. The purpose of trademark law is to (1) protect sellers' reputations, (2) prevent consumer confusion and deception regarding providers of goods and services, and (3) promote competition (U.S. Senate, 1946). Trademark law accomplishes these goals by granting exclusive rights to a business to use particular marks to identify its goods or services. Unlike patents and copyrights, trademarks are not authorized under the Constitution's IP clause. Instead, Congress's power to regulate interstate commerce is the source of authority for federal trademark law.[15]

Under a 1946 act to provide for the registration and protection of trademarks used in commerce, commonly known as the Lanham Act, any "word, name, symbol, or device or any combination thereof" may be used as a trademark "to indicate the source of" goods or services (Pub. L. 79-489). Examples include brand names and logos, such as *Nike*, the familiar swoosh, and the "Just Do It" slogan. The mark must be distinctive enough to permit consumers to associate a product with a specific source, so a vague or generic term is not protected. Trademark law organizes terms on a spectrum of distinctiveness, which is

---

[15] A federal trademark must be "used in commerce" before it can be registered (15 U.S.C. 1051[a]), and the term *commerce* refers to interstate commerce that Congress can regulate (15 U.S.C. 1127).

divided into five categories (*Abercrombie & Fitch Co. v. Hunting World, Inc.*, 1976 [providing useful definitions for types of marks in the spectrum of distinctiveness]):

- A *generic* word defines a product or service, such as *phone* or *pizza*. These words are never given trademark protection because no one can have an exclusive right to use common words.
- A *descriptive* term merely describes an associated product or service. Such terms are generally not eligible for trademark protection. But if a descriptive term acquires a *secondary meaning* in the market such that consumers immediately associate the term with a specific business, it becomes protectable. For instance, *New Haven Pizza* is a nonprotectable descriptive term, but *Kentucky Fried Chicken* is protected because it has acquired a secondary meaning among restaurant customers.
- A *suggestive* mark alludes to a characteristic of a product or service. For instance, *Microsoft* is suggestive of software and microcomputers.
- An *arbitrary* mark involves using a common word in an unfamiliar way to identify a product. An example is *Apple* in the world of personal technology.
- A *fanciful* term is a word "invented solely for [its] use" as a trademark.

In sum, suggestive, arbitrary, and fanciful marks are considered "inherently distinctive" and are therefore entitled to trademark protection. Contrastingly, generic terms are not distinctive and do not enjoy protection. Finally, descriptive terms are generally not inherently distinctive, but they can become distinctive if they acquire a secondary meaning, through which consumers associate the term with a specific source of goods or services. If this dynamic is clearly established, a descriptive term can become eligible for trademark protection.

Trademark protection is not limited to words and phrases and can include patterns (e.g., the Nike swoosh) and sounds (e.g., the NBC bell tone). The U.S. Supreme Court has held that even a color can be a valid trademark under the Lanham Act if it somehow acquires secondary meaning to permit identification (*Qualitex Co. v. Jacobson Prods. Co.*, 1995). However, certain types of marks cannot be eligible. The most important of these are the functional aspects of a product or service. The doctrine of functionality bars trademark protection for such aspects because, "[i]f a product's functional features could be used as trademarks . . . , a monopoly over such features could be obtained" (*Qualitex*, 1995; see also *Apple Inc. v. Samsung Elecs. Co.*, 2015 [holding that certain design features on the iPhone were utilitarian and were therefore not entitled to trademark protection]), thereby circumventing patent law. The functionality doctrine applies to both aesthetic features and utilitarian ones, thus preventing businesses from monopolizing eye-catching designs (*ERBE Elektromedizin GmbH v. Canady Tech. LLC*, 2010). The doctrine also limits the scope of valid trademarks. For instance, although a shoe designer can enjoy protection for distinctive red-soled shoes, the designer cannot obtain and possess exclusive rights for an entirely red shoe (*Christian Louboutin S.A. v. Yves Saint Laurent Am. Holding, Inc.*, 2012).

Any organization—including a federal agency—can obtain a trademark by registering an eligible mark with the USPTO.[16] The registration can be renewed indefinitely but is valid only if the mark is continuously used in commerce activities. Trademark holders have the right to prevent other businesses from using the same or substantially similar marks and can sue to enforce that right. The key question in such lawsuits is whether the alleged infringing use of a mark causes confusion among ordinary customers regarding the source or affiliation of goods or services (15 U.S.C. 1114). If so, the trademark holder can obtain an injunction to prevent further usage of the infringing mark, as well as to be awarded compensation. This has dual implications for DHS: It can both enforce its trademarks and be enjoined from using others' trademarks.

DHS faces trademark issues in several instances. Government programs often use logos, mottos, and special names for various initiatives. E-Verify, Global Entry, the Customs Trade Partnership Against Terrorism [CTPAT], and the National Flood Insurance Program are

---

[16] Limited common law rights might be available without registration.

examples (each is described in more detail in the appendix). Often, DHS programs' logos are not trademarked and are therefore not protected from appropriation by others. In fact, unlike the Secret Service has for its seal, for example, DHS lacks statutory protection for the DHS seal, which would empower the department to take action against abusers of the symbol. Third parties, which often seek financial gain, are engaged in activities that can confuse the public by misusing government program materials. DHS does seek trademark protection and pursues enforcement actions against abusers; however, this practice is not routinely done at the programmatic level at present.

Intellectual Property in Acquisition Law

DHS's procurement and acquisition activities are inherently tied to the use and purchase of others' IP, particularly in the form of software and data. Acquisition laws and regulations spell out in great detail the contractual terms used in government purchasing. Technical data and computer software are species of IP unique to federal acquisition law. Within the context of acquisitions, *technical data* is defined as "recorded information (regardless of the method of recording) of a scientific of technical nature" about items or services delivered to the government pursuant to a procurement contract (41 U.S.C. 116; Federal Acquisition Regulation [FAR] 52.227-14). These data can be valuable to the government for installation, operation, repair, maintenance, upgrade, and replacement. Incidentally, this data resource is also extremely valuable to the contractor as a trade secret.[17]

---

[17] A trade secret is a type of IP and can include any type of proprietary technical or nontechnical information. Two requirements must be met: (1) The owner must take reasonable efforts to keep the information secret, and (2) the information's secrecy must generate economic value. See 18 U.S.C. 1836. Historically, trade secrets have been governed by state law, but, in 2016, Congress passed the Defend Trade Secrets Act, which created a federal cause of action for misappropriation of trade secrets (Pub. L. 114-153, as codified at 18 U.S.C. 1836). DHS is immune to suits under the act (18 U.S.C. 1833[a][1]), but it might be contractually obligated to protect contractors' trade secrets under nondisclosure agreements.

Although a contractor is obligated to deliver any technical data called for by its procurement contract, the government does receive ownership of the IP for the data when contracting under the FAR.[18] The government obtains *unlimited rights* under a license agreement to utilize the data "in any manner and for any purpose" with respect to (1) data produced in performing the contract; (2) form, fit, and function data; and (3) data necessary for routine operations, maintenance, installation, training, and repair (FAR 52.227-14).[19] With regard to usage of the data in other functions, the government is entitled to only *limited rights* (FAR 52.227-14). The government may use and reproduce limited rights data internally but may not share the data with outside entities without the contractor's approval (FAR 52.227-14).[20] The government may, however, negotiate to obtain prior approval to disclose limited-rights data under predefined conditions (see FAR 52.227-14 Alternate II).

Technical data specifically excludes computer software delivered under procurement contracts, which is governed under a similar IP scheme. Like it does with technical data, the government obtains *unlimited rights* to software produced in performance of the contract. If the software was developed at private expense, however, the government obtains a license for restrictive rights: The government may use the software on only one computer per license and may not share the software with the IP owner's competitors.[21]

DHS is a major purchaser of software and support from contractors and other vendors. As a result, the IP dimensions of procurement programs are nearly universal and require a high degree of competency in IP strategy and procurement law. As we document in this report,

---

[18] DHS uses a variety of procurement contracts, including other transactions and inter-agency agreements, to send funds to other agencies to put on contract. These processes are not as formalized as the FAR, and the IP terms are less established.

[19] The contractor can generally assert copyright protection for academic articles based on data delivered with unlimited rights.

[20] Defense acquisition is governed by a slightly different scheme under 10 U.S.C. 2320 and its implementing regulations.

[21] Service contractors may access the software to diagnose and correct errors.

DHS has many procurement specialists, but few have a broad perspective and experience with the IP dimensions of their acquisition programs.

The Invention Secrecy Act

As mentioned in the introduction to this report, DHS is planning how to implement patent application reviews for national security risk per the ISA. A follow-on report for DHS officials will provide a deeper review of the act and its implementation. For current purposes, we briefly review the history and purpose of the act as another dimension of IP that DHS has to manage.

The ISA was passed in the aftermath of World War II. The act granted the U.S. government the authority to limit the disclosure of information contained in patent applications in cases in which such disclosure was deemed to be detrimental to U.S. national security (35 U.S.C. 181). A critical component of the act is the secrecy order, which is issued by the commissioner of patents in the USPTO. Upon determining that public disclosure of an invention could jeopardize U.S. national security, the commissioner must "order that the invention be kept secret and withhold the publication of the application or the grant of a patent" (35 U.S.C. 181). In fiscal year 2018, the USPTO placed 5,792 patent applications under secrecy orders.[22]

Overall, an essential feature of the patent system is that the inventor discloses and explains how the invention works and what it can do (World Intellectual Property Organization, undated). Through the publication of the patent application, information contained in patents becomes visible to the greater public, including foreign adversaries of the United States (Maune, 2012, pp. 471–472). When determining whether a secrecy order should be issued, USPTO officials must weigh the U.S. government's national security interests against the inventor's right to exclude others from making, using, or selling the invention (Maune, 2012, pp. 471–472; USPTO, 2015).

---

[22] Information provided directly to RAND by USPTO.

History

The ISA was not the first law of its kind. The act follows an act of 1917 that expired at the conclusion of World War I. That act outlined that, in the event that an invention was deemed to be

> detrimental to the public safety or defense, or may assist the enemy or endanger the successful prosecution of the war, [the Commissioner of Patents] may order that the invention be kept secret and withhold the grant of a patent until the end of the war. (Pub. L. 65-80, 1917)

The act was renewed in 1940 as preparatory measure for the United States' entrance into World War II (Pub. L. 76-700, 1940; Lee, 1997, pp. 345, 349–350) and was amended a year later to include stricter penalties for violations of secrecy orders (Lee, 1997, p. 350).

By 1951, the United States had entered the Korean War. Consequently, the U.S. Department of Defense (DoD) demanded that Congress grant it continued invention-secrecy powers through the ISA (Lee, 1997, p. 352). The 1951 act differed from its predecessors in multiple ways (Lee, 1997, pp. 352–353, noting that changes in the ISA provided mechanisms for compensation for inventors and prevented inventors from filing patent applications outside the United States within six months of filing in the United States without a license from the Secretary of Commerce)—most noticeably in that it extended authority of invention-secrecy orders to peacetime (Lee, 1997, p. 352). The previous invention-secrecy acts effectively operated during wartime, thus marking a noticeable change in policy (Lee, 1997, p. 352).

The Impact of a Secrecy Order

An established secrecy order remains in effect as long as a government agency determines that the national interest requires that it remain in place. Like other patent applications, patent applications with secrecy orders must be evaluated for patentability (*Manual of Patent Examining Procedure* [MPEP] [USPTO, 2013], § 130). When the commissioner determines that an application with a secrecy order qualifies for a patent, the USPTO issues a notice of allowability, which precludes or ends prosecution of the application (MPEP § 130). If already underway, the prosecution of the application is halted until the secrecy order is rescinded (MPEP § 130). A secrecy order ends either when it is not renewed or when the sponsoring agency informs the USPTO that the order is no longer required (35 U.S.C. 181). When a secrecy order has been rescinded, the USPTO issues a notice of allowance to the inventor, signaling that it intends to issue a patent (37 C.F.R. § 5.3[c]).

Policy Considerations in the Implementation of the Invention Secrecy Act

Although ISA reviews are required by statute, they are not without their critics. We raise some of the criticisms here as background information for DHS decisionmakers. Various scholars have argued that secrecy orders that are established in peacetime are not justifiable given "minimal findings on modern circumstances that necessitate such a policy" (Lee, 1997, p. 354). The scholars add that secrecy orders are detrimental to innovation, imposing limitations on private parties who are prevented from fully enjoying the financial benefits of their creations (Katich, 2015, pp. 413, 419). Others have also suggested that the ISA could, in specific instances, constitute a taking of private property for "public use," which is unconstitutional under the Fifth Amendment.[23]

Additionally, scientists have contended that ISA secrecy orders have become overused. The Federation of American Scientists argues that government agencies "err on the side of caution and impose secrecy orders on patents that present even the slightest threats" (Dilawar, 2018).

Although secrecy orders are rarely issued, they can place a burden on inventors' rights, drawing criticism from both scholars and scientists. However, underlying the imposition of the secrecy order is the primacy of the United States' national security, which the U.S. government has valued as its most important priority—even during peace-

---

[23] See, e.g., Lee, 1997, p. 407:

Despite the uncertainties surrounding some of the case law as to whether a taking claim is available for the imposition of a secrecy order, the very nature of the regulation, especially when accompanied by government use, strongly supports that such a claim should be recognized.

time. Under the ISA, the inventor's rights have been deemed worth sacrificing, thus exemplifying a unique tension between the American ideals of promoting innovation and ensuring that the United States remains safe from its adversaries.

Summary

This chapter is intended to give the novice reader a broad understanding of IP concepts and the major areas of IP law. These areas are representative of the type of work that DHS and component IP attorneys can manage on behalf of DHS clients. This chapter also identifies some particular areas of concern for DHS, such as the impacts and implications of implementing the ISA.

IP is a specialized function that requires attention, but, as we demonstrate in Chapters Three and Four, it has not been fully developed at an institutional level for maximum support to missions, operations, and overall departmental success. In Chapter Three, we move to provide an understanding of the DHS structure, components, and mission sets. Then, we turn to the highlighting the ways in which IP is directly related to improving risk management and the full mission functions of DHS and component programs.

Department of Homeland Security Missions and Intellectual Property Management

DHS missions and objectives are diverse, involved, and interconnected. Following its formation in 2002, DHS merged 22 distinct entities under the umbrella of one organization. To unify the wide variety of homeland security responsibilities entrusted to each of the new components, the department developed overarching mission goals to focus the efforts of these previously disparate entities. Seventeen years later, DHS serves an important role in acting as the glue that binds these various components together in a cohesive mission.

In this chapter, we review DHS missions and objectives to provide an understanding of how the institution has formed its current approach to management of IP activities. The goal of the chapter is to describe the role that IP assets play within DHS and in support of homeland security. The chapter begins by providing an overview of the overarching missions and objectives of DHS, then moves on to discuss the unique functions of individual agency components. The chapter proceeds to discuss the current structure and management of IP matters at the department and component levels.

Department of Homeland Security: Background and Missions

Congress created DHS on November 25, 2002, and the department commenced operations on March 1, 2003. It was formed after the attacks of September 11, 2001, and sought to bring together U.S. internal security capabilities to prevent similar attacks on U.S. soil in the future. Congress created, shifted, and reorganized several individual departments to be included under the umbrella of DHS. As a result, multiple organizations came together to collectively meet in accomplishing the mission goals of homeland security. Given the overwhelming task of bringing these distinct parts together, the department has since developed several principal missions, objectives, and goals to help form a common vision to support and drive all components of DHS.

The Homeland Security Act of 2002 provided the following elements of the primary mission of the new agency:

> (A) prevent terrorist attacks within the United States; (B) reduce the vulnerability of the United States to terrorism; (C) minimize the damage, and assist in the recovery, from terrorist attacks that do occur within the United States; (D) carry out all functions of entities transferred to the Department, including by acting as a focal point regarding natural and manmade crises and emergency planning; (E) ensure that the functions of the agencies and subdivisions within the Department that are not related directly to securing the homeland are not diminished or neglected except by a specific explicit Act of Congress; (F) ensure that the overall economic security of the United States is not diminished by efforts, activities, and programs aimed at securing the homeland; and (G) monitor connections between illegal drug trafficking and terrorism, coordinate efforts to sever such connections, and otherwise contribute to efforts to interdict illegal drug trafficking. (Pub. L. 107-296, § 101)

Department of Homeland Security Components: Background

Several operational and support components carry out core DHS missions. Many of the operational components existed in some form prior to being integrated to the department in 2003. The support components were restructured to assist the department at the headquarter level, receiving their missions and tasks in the Homeland Security Act of 2002. The nine operational components of DHS are

- U.S. Customs and Border Protection (CBP)
- CISA
- FEMA
- Federal Law Enforcement Training Center (FLETC)
- U.S. Immigration and Customs Enforcement (ICE)
- TSA
- U.S. Coast Guard (USCG)
- U.S. Citizenship and Immigration Services (USCIS)
- U.S. Secret Service.

The department's five support components are

- Countering Weapons of Mass Destruction (WMD) Office (CWMD)
- Management Directorate
- Office of Intelligence and Analysis
- Office of Operations Coordination
- S&T.

In addition to the overall DHS missions, each operational component has identified and defined unique goals and related objectives that align with its new and preexisting organizational responsibilities. These specific activities remain in alignment with the overall missions defined by the department, ensuring that all components are working toward the same overarching outcomes.

The 2010 Quadrennial Homeland Security Review

From these directives, DHS cultivated a foundational mission. Two documents have been critical in the historical and ongoing development of DHS's vision, mission, and goals: the Quadrennial Homeland Security Review (QHSR) and the DHS strategic plan. These reports are complementary, with the QHSR establishing the missions and overall strategic approach to those missions and the strategic plan developing the specific milestones and objectives needed to succeed in the core missions.

The first QHSR, published in 2010, took the opportunity to reflect on the agency's first eight years and more clearly dictate the future mission (DHS, 2010). To establish future goals, the report described the foundational concepts and vision for the department. The concepts "form the foundation for a comprehensive approach to homeland security" (DHS, 2010, p. ix). Consequently, these ideas are not limited to DHS but should ultimately inform a general, basic understanding of homeland security for use across the government. The three foundational concepts also provide a base for the department's five missions. The foundational concepts are as follows:

- **security:** This concept is defined as protecting the United States and its people, vital interests, and way of life. Aspects of security include preventing and deterring attacks, identifying and stopping threats, denying hostile actors from working within borders, and protecting the nation's infrastructure. DHS and the broader homeland security enterprise must work to prevent threats along supply chains that are interconnected and used for unlawful, as well as lawful, purposes (DHS, 2010, p. 15).
- **resilience:** This concept is defined as fostering individual, community, and system robustness, adaptability, and capacity for rapid recovery. With the world increasingly interconnected by networks, providing great benefit to the lives and prosperity of Americans, there are more points of vulnerability for the United States. Knowing that the United States will face the threat of attacks, challenges, and disasters, its government must develop a more resilient nation that can recover from these challenges with increasing ease (DHS, 2010, pp. 15–16).
- **customs and exchange:** This concept is defined as expediting and enforcing lawful trade, travel, and immigration. The department recognizes the need to work with partners and stakeholders to move goods and people through U.S. transportation systems safely. The intent is to embed security and safety into U.S. "global movement systems, so that movement systems and customs and

exchange are mutually reinforcing against possible problems and vulnerabilities" (DHS, 2010, p. 16).

Department of Homeland Security Missions

Building from these concepts, the QHSR developed a vision and set of missions for the homeland security enterprise. The DHS homeland security vision encompasses "a homeland that is safe, secure, and resilient against terrorism and other hazards, where American interests, aspirations, and way of life can thrive" (DHS, 2010, p. 4).

Figure 3.1 shows DHS's five operational missions and the one departmental mission. We then describe these six overall missions and their supporting goals.

Prevent Terrorism and Enhance Security

The three goals in this mission are as follows:

- Prevent terrorist attacks.
- Prevent unauthorized acquisition, importation, movement, or use of chemical, biological, radiological, and nuclear materials and capabilities within the United States.
- Reduce the vulnerability that critical infrastructure, key resources, essential leadership, and major events have to terrorist attacks and other hazards (DHS, 2016c).

The mission of preventing terrorism and enhancing security is viewed as the founding principle and highest priority for DHS. This mission comes directly from the Homeland Security Act of 2002. In the act, Congress states that the first three facets of the department's mission will be to "prevent terrorist attacks within the United States, reduce the vulnerability of the United States to terrorism, and minimize the damage, and assist in the recovery, from terrorist attacks that do occur within the United States" (Pub. L. 107-296, § 101). Despite the principal nature of this "first" mission, the department and the QHSR have recognized that this undertaking cannot be the sole focus for DHS in terms of strengthening homeland security. The threats and concerns that have emerged in the 17 years since the creation of DHS

Figure 3.1
Department of Homeland Security Operational and Departmental Missions

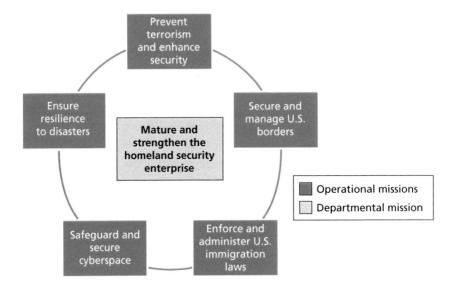

have shown the need for a broader conception of homeland security. Thus, the department developed the following additional missions and supporting goals:

- Secure and manage U.S. borders.
  - Effectively secure U.S. air, land, and sea points of entry.
  - Safeguard and streamline lawful trade and travel.
  - Disrupt and dismantle transnational criminal and terrorist organizations (DHS, 2016b).
- Enforce and administer U.S. immigration laws.
  - Strengthen and effectively administer the immigration system.
  - Prevent unlawful immigration (DHS, 2018d).
- Safeguard and secure cyberspace.
  - Strengthen the security and resilience of critical infrastructure.
  - Secure the federal civilian government information technology enterprise.
  - Advance law enforcement, incident response, and reporting capabilities.

- Strengthen the ecosystem (DHS, 2018c).
- Ensure resilience to disasters.
    - Enhance national preparedness.
    - Mitigate hazards and responsibilities.
    - Ensure effective emergency response.
    - Enable rapid recovery (DHS, 2016a).
- Mature and strengthen the homeland security enterprise.
    - Integrate intelligence, information sharing, and operations.
    - Enhance partnerships and outreach.
    - Conduct homeland security R&D.
    - Train and exercise frontline operators and first responders.
    - Strengthen service delivery and manage DHS resources (DHS, 2016d).

Current Structure and Management of Intellectual Property

Currently, DHS operates a federated approach to IP management, with centralized IP management at the secretary level. Under this model, each of DHS's 22 subordinate agencies and offices implements component-level IP functions (see generally J. Johnson, 2014). Furthermore, the secretary has delegated responsibility for IP management and support to three headquarters offices (see Ridge, 2004, and Chertoff, 2005). **S&T** establishes and manages the DHS IP programs "for the entire Department," including entering into cooperative research and development agreements (CRADAs), licensing DHS IP, managing department inventions, and implementing the Federal Technology Transfer Act of 1986 (Pub. L. 99-502).

Second, **OGC** provides counsel on all legal matters concerning DHS IP programs. This includes establishing IP policy and interacting with DHS components, other agencies, and external entities to identify, obtain, and maintain IP rights on DHS's behalf. OGC created the Technology Programs Law Division (TPLD) to accomplish the organization's delegated responsibilities (see TPLD, 2018). Led by the associate general counsel and the deputy associate general counsel,

TPLD consists of two subgroups: the Science and Technology Group and OGC/IP. The mission of TPLD is to provide legal support for science and technology and IP matters across the five core DHS missions (see Figure 3.1). The principal group for the purposes of this study is OGC/IP, led by the assistant general counsel for IP.

In the past, several DHS components have detailed personnel in OGC/IP to facilitate interactions between S&T, OGC, and their home agencies. However, the length and scope of these assignments vary, and subordinate agencies are not required to provide staff to TPLD. Funding for these positions is provided by the sending agency, which leaves TPLD and S&T with neither the authority nor the resources to make the positions permanent. The remaining mechanism for TPLD's interaction with DHS component and support agencies is through contact with agency-based personnel whom the individual agencies have designated as IP points of contact (POCs).

Third, the **chief procurement officer**, in consultation with the general counsel, provides guidance on IP related to contracts, financial assistance, reimbursable agreements, and other like instruments.

Notwithstanding the above delegations, the relationships between the three offices and the remaining component and support agencies are not defined or delineated pursuant to any DHS policy, memorandum, instruction, or directive. The sole reference to the relationship between the three offices and the rest of the department is the general counsel's responsibility to counsel on IP programs and interact with DHS components (OGC, 2010).

The Department of Homeland Security Directive 012-01: Intellectual Property Framework

DHS Directive 012-01 (OGC, 2010) mandates that OGC "be consulted" with regard to employee inventions. Department employees and contractors are required to report their inventions for guidance from OGC/IP attorneys through the IP process. Similarly, DHS employees are required to "consult" with OGC with regard to the use of patented, copyrighted, and trademarked materials, as well as the use of any data owned by others that contain any restrictions. Additionally, Directive 012-01 assigns liabilities for costs, fees, and damages to the component of the employee responsible for any IP infringement or violation.

Directive 012-01 does not contain a section establishing the IP responsibilities of component or support agency heads or their designees.[1] Moreover, the overall relationship between component and support agency heads and S&T and OGC is left undefined. For example, agency heads do not have any reporting requirements to S&T, OGC, or any other secretariat-level official with regard to IP management activities. Thus, the IP management framework constructed by Directive 012-01 created 19 individual subagency approaches to IP management and programs. As a result, many DHS agencies do not have an existing IP program or designated personnel assigned to respond to IP matters. Contrastingly, some agencies possess a vested interest in a particular aspect of IP (e.g., USCG's protection of its trademarks or FEMA's protection of its trademarks)[2] and have maintained more-robust programs with designated legal personnel.

Characteristics of the Federated Approach to Intellectual Property Management

Intellectual Property at Department of Homeland Security Headquarters

Directive 012-01 has resulted in the implementation of a federated structure of governance and management of IP at DHS. This governance structure is characterized by a centralized authority composed of S&T, OGC (TPLD), and (to a much lesser extent) the chief procurement officer. This central authority has little or no established (doc-

---

[1] Within DHS, a directive does not delegate responsibilities to an official or office. The purpose of a DHS directive is to briefly and broadly articulate and build on DHS policy statements, policies, missions, programs, activities, or business practices of a continuing nature that are required or authorized by statute, rulemaking, the President, or the Secretary to initiate, govern, or regulate actions or conduct by DHS components, officers, and employees. See Office of the Deputy Under Secretary for Management, 2008. Thus, components and support agencies do not have specifically delegated responsibilities, authorities, or powers from the Secretary of DHS.

[2] See Chapter Four and the appendix for component summaries and a more detailed description of individual agencies' equities in particular IP domains (e.g., patent, trademark, copyright).

umented) command and control over the DHS subordinate entities that execute IP programs, tasks, oversight, and so on. Each component represents a constituent IP authority that maintains relative autonomy with respect to its own internal IP management.

In the absence of DHS guidance clearly delineating the duties, roles, and responsibilities between the headquarters IP authority and the subordinate agencies, TPLD has attempted to clarify the relationships.[3] For example, TPLD tried to institute a series of memoranda of understanding with the components in order to define which IP services TPLD would provide and the resulting fees the components would reimburse S&T for those services (e.g., patent filings, trademark violation disputes). This effort was largely unsuccessful, however, because the components were not obligated to enter into such agreements and had not budgeted for the payment of such fees in return for IP support from TPLD.

In 2016, the director of the Office of Public–Private Partnerships, Deputy Under Secretary for S&T, issued a memorandum entitled, "Intellectual Property, Technology Transfer and Commercialization Governance, Implementation and Metrics Plan" (Director, Office of Public–Private Partnerships, 2016). This internal S&T memorandum defined the responsibilities, planning, and tracking mechanisms that exist with regard to the function and interaction of the Office of Public–Private Partnerships' Technology Transfer and Commercialization Program and OGC. The memo described how the two offices would manage all IP issues that relate to the program (e.g., contracting, licensing, CRADAs, copyrights, memoranda of understanding). This detailed memo addressed how the two offices would coordinate requirements throughout the life cycle of a particular IP asset or issue. Moreover, it defined metrics to determine and assess outcomes, which would then be used to resource each office's staffing, training, and education. This memorandum appears to be the only delineation of governance-related operating procedures that exists between OGC and another office or agency within DHS.

---

[3]   HSOAC interviews with TPLD leadership and staff, as well as interviews with DHS component personnel.

According to what we learned in our interviews, since approximately 2010, the relationship between headquarters IP and each of the components has been individualized because of the unique needs of particular agencies. For example, when USCG or ICE needs a patent to be filed, it can request assistance from TPLD. This assistance is not required, however. Components are free to file patents and such on their own. However, in most instances, they are unlikely to do so, given the low numbers of IP-trained attorneys at the components. Similarly, if USCIS or another agency wishes to file a trademark for a certain program, it is likely to request support from TPLD. In contrast, other components (e.g., CBP and CISA) are more likely to take on some of these functions in house because they have IP-trained staff attorneys. The individualized relationships are further supported through a system in which several components provide or detail attorneys to TPLD to assist the office in meeting its specific IP needs. These personnel, however, are retained in that role at the discretion of the sending agency. Seven component-level attorneys, including all six IP-specialized component-funded attorneys, are currently detailed to TPLD part time.

Intellectual Property Staffing and Functions at the Department of Homeland Security and the Components

In terms of general staffing levels, at TPLD, there is currently one assistant general counsel funded by OGC headquarters. In addition, S&T funds six full-time attorney-advisers, five contractors (providing patent and paralegal services), and two paralegals. The six S&T-funded full-time attorney-advisers support litigation actions, dispute resolution, and enforcement activities and manage the patent and trademark prosecution portfolios. They additionally support technology-transfer initiatives, manage licenses and support to the International Cooperative Programs Office, and assist with multiple procurement activities for DHS-level R&D and procurement divisions.

At the component level, only nine agencies currently maintain staff dedicated to some degree of IP management–related duties.[4] The

---

[4] We selected and interviewed people from nine subordinate agencies for this research. Our selection of these nine subordinate agencies was driven by the information that TPLD gave us. TPLD reported that these nine agencies had the most-developed and robust IP programs

staff duties vary by component, based on the IP needs of the programs and on the presence of IP-specialized staff (see the appendix for detailed descriptions of component IP activities). At the time we wrote this report, the components had the following in-house IP support:

- CBP: three IP-specialized attorneys
- CISA: one IP-specialized attorney
- FEMA: one IP-specialized attorney
- FLETC: one procurement attorney serving as the POC on IP
- ICE: one procurement attorney serving as the POC on IP
- TSA: one IP-specialized attorney
- USCG: one attorney working part time on IP
- USCIS: one attorney working part time on IP.

We conducted interviews with people from these nine agencies and found that each entity retains at least one dedicated attorney within its chief counsel's office who is the notional POC for addressing IP-related matters. These attorneys occupy full-time-equivalent positions that the component owns and for which the component budgets, leaving those positions' functions vulnerable to adjustments in agency-specific priorities.

Given this workforce structure and alignment, agency IP attorneys are principally responsible for addressing IP needs related to their particular agency's mission sets. Our research has found that these specific needs range across the following categories:

- patents (filing, litigation, enforcement)
- trademarks and copyrights (registration, enforcement)
- procurement and contracts
  - data rights
  - licenses
  - subscriptions
- ISA compliance (a planned activity for DHS)

---

within DHS or that personnel in these agencies were most likely to interact with, and rely on, TPLD for IP services and support. For the purposes of this study, we did not reach out to the remaining 12 agencies, directorates, or offices.

- coordination and management of CRADAs and international agreements.

Our interviews revealed that the activities in which IP attorneys engaged largely surrounded IP needs as they came about during particular agency operations. For example, the FEMA attorney handling IP matters works full time on resolving IP issues largely related to litigation for patent infringement. By virtue of the fact that FEMA is involved in more IP disputes than other components are, the attorney spends a majority of time on litigation and related tasks (e.g., reviewing claims against the government in instances of infringement and assisting the U.S. Department of Justice [DOJ] in defending against those actions). However, the attorney handling IP issues for USCIS is rarely involved with IP litigation and dedicates much less time (approximately 10 percent of duty time) to IP issues. Instead, the attorney dedicated much more time to reviewing copyright compliance, trademark registration requests, and procurement and contract issues. In the appendix, we examine each subordinate agency with regard to the categories of IP that are of concern, as well as the level of effort expended for each.

In general, we found that the nine agencies expressed a consistent concern over prioritizing procurement and contracting issues and devoted a significant amount of time to this category of work. Legal review is triggered for bids that exceed certain contracting thresholds (ranging from $500,000 to $5 million, depending on the type of acquisition). Agency attorneys reviewing these contracts need to ensure that they contain language and sections that protect DHS IP rights. Agency attorneys consistently stressed the importance of data-rights clauses that protect DHS use of and control over software and system-related data sets that are collected or managed by vendors and their products. Failures in ensuring proper data-right protections has led to vendor disputes, increased costs, and even litigation. Similarly, licensing and subscription conditions must be reviewed so that DHS personnel properly access and use only the systems, programs, and information that the department has contracted and purchased. The failure to include the appropriate language has been costly for DHS agencies and, in some cases, diminished mission effectiveness.

Summary

This chapter grounds the remainder of the report in the mission areas of DHS overall and of the components. DHS's unique history presents inherent challenges to implementation and maintenance of a department-level IP coordination function. The future success of the coordinating function will be connected to several factors: (1) the ability of OGC/IP and S&T to articulate the importance of IP in overarching mission functions, (2) appropriate resourcing, (3) appropriately delegated authorities, (4) component IP integration efforts with OGC/IP and S&T, and (5) integration with the Office of Procurement Operations. Understanding those mission functions and the current IP management structure provides a stable launching point for the discussion in Chapter Four. In Chapter Four, we discuss the ways in which IP can be better managed to advance DHS goals, enhance the components, and increase mission success.

A Framework for Intellectual Property Supporting Department of Homeland Security Missions

In Chapter Three, we outlined the diverse mission areas that DHS and the components pursue as they collectively work to ensure homeland security. In this chapter, we provide a more explicit link between those mission sets and their underlying IP needs, functions, opportunities, and pitfalls. Examining the IP issues that are often under the surface will demonstrate how and when an IP program can deliver benefits to mission success or how and when a failure to consider and effectively manage IP matters can pose a risk to missions, programs, and progress.

We begin with a notional framework for conceptualizing the risk–reward trade-offs when IP is either neglected or actively incorporated into mission planning and operations. Following the framework, we provide a series of vignettes culled from the interviews we conducted with DHS and component staff related to IP management as currently practiced at the department (within the structure of authorities and responsibilities introduced in Chapter Three). We have kept this framework at a high level to categorize the types of risks and benefits that DHS can face when different types of IP are involved. Our concept breakdowns are meant to show DHS leaders a set of common representative problems, issues, and options that have arisen when IP matters present clear operational or mission-important challenges. The list of vignettes is intended to be representative, not comprehensive. Given the fact that most of the components do not retain dedicated, IP-trained staff attorneys, there are more opportunities in which IP can provide additional support in mitigating or eliminating challenges to mission success.

A Framework for Understanding Intellectual Property–Related Risks

In Chapter Three, we outlined the mission areas that DHS and the components serve and introduced how the department and the components are currently addressing IP issues. DHS only recently began explicitly focusing on IP matters, starting to staff headquarters around 2009. Since then, TPLD has grown to seven full-time attorneys, and the components have begun to recognize their own interests in managing IP resources by establishing POCs for IP matters or hiring their own IP-specialized attorneys. The latter programs are particularly new developments, with the longest-established IP program in the components having been stood up about six years ago.

This recent growth in IP interest, driven in part by the complexity of procurement and increasing technological reliance, has demonstrated the need for IP programming as a support function at DHS. But viewing IP activities as a support function misses much of the value that IP provides to mission success. This chapter argues for a different perspective, one that moves IP from a support function to a mission-enabling asset—with associated risks, harms, and benefits that can be managed to enhance mission goals or mismanaged to present avoidable obstacles to success.

By characterizing the current state of IP activity at DHS as a support function, we mean that IP is not routinely viewed as an asset that advances mission success but rather as an ancillary activity, like accounting or purchasing. Because IP activities are rarely operational in nature,[1] IP has not been directly incorporated into mission planning and strategic positioning.

We believe that this arrangement does not serve the department's long-term interests because it underutilizes IP as a strategic asset that can reveal new strengths and weakness in department programming,

---

[1] Compare this with, for instance, CBP and ICE's IP enforcement responsibilities, including ICE's HSI-led National Intellectual Property Rights Coordination Center (National Intellectual Property Rights Coordination Center, undated b). Note, however, that our research indicates that neither CBP nor ICE has an IP attorney advising on IP rights and responsibilities in the area of IP enforcement.

help actively manage mission risks, and help position the department as an innovative agency that both creates and deploys IP and technology more broadly in service to the nation. Moving IP management from a support function to a mission asset can enhance the success, efficiency, or effectiveness of DHS programs and operations. This transition requires an understanding of the benefits and risks associated with reliance on and effective use of IP assets. This matter is the perspective we elicited in the introductory chapter, in which the emergency directive from the CISA director issued a clarion call to immediate action to defend against DNS tampering. In that example, CISA did not explicitly recognize the direct role that IP attorney staff could have played in initiating the DNS dispute-resolution process at ICANN— a quasi-regulatory grievance system that likely would have shut down fake domains and could have additionally resulted in information sharing, awareness raising, and real-time monitoring of the types of behavior of immediate concern to the department and the government at large. We recognize that this specific incident is not the only example of DHS IP assets being discounted in times of need. Furthermore, we are not criticizing the actions and decisions of any individuals during the crisis. However, the immediate lesson from this example is that IP operational capabilities have not regularly risen to the appropriate level of attention. This oversight is an omission of capability awareness, not of value.

To help illustrate the ways in which IP can help or hinder missions, we created a notional framework to introduce leadership to the value locked within IP asset management. We began by identifying a series of risk categories that classify common dimensions of concern that program managers ought to consider:

- **reputational risk:** the potential that adverse publicity regarding the institutional practices and associations—whether accurate or not—will cause a loss of confidence in the integrity of the institution as a whole[2]

---

2   Adapted from Basel Committee on Banking Supervision, 2001.

- **operational risk:** the direct or indirect loss resulting from inadequate or failed internal processes, people, and systems or from external events[3]
- **credibility risk:** the degree to which communications are believed and trusted by the customers, clients, and communities that the institution serves
- **innovation risk:** the degree to which creating or failing to create new designs, technologies, systems, processes, and capabilities can affect mission accomplishment
- **financial or litigation risk:** the direct or indirect loss of budgetary resources and the risk of exposure to lawsuits that absorb institutional resources.

Along these five dimensions of risk, a program manager either implicitly or explicitly chooses to deploy assets that will balance risk with reward in service to program success. Although many of these dimensions are regularly and routinely considered as part of program risk evaluation, some assets (such as IP) are overlooked as a matter of course. It is this area of overlooked program assets (IP matters) that presents a series of risks that we hope to illuminate with this framework.

Consider a program manager's decision to partner with an outside firm to deliver security monitoring at a government building. The program manager's decision on whom to hire (and for what functions) will have implications for the reputational risk of the program. Forming partnerships with disreputable, untested, or otherwise uncommitted firms would harm the government program's overall institutional reputation. In contrast, effective selection of partnerships can produce positive benefits that enhance reputation (perhaps because the chosen firm is known for efficiency, innovation, or public spiritedness).

Operational risks, similarly, are managed with the resilience and sustainability of processes in mind. An example would be the administration of a particular supply chain by a program manager. Disruptions to supply chains; overreliance on a limited number of critical products, skill sets, or personnel; economic and political fluctuations; and mis-

---

[3]   Adapted from Basel Committee on Banking Supervision, 2001.

judgments in the available demand for program assets all represent the types of operational risks that program managers must consider. Preparing in advance for disruptions, redundancies in suppliers, pipelines of talent acquisition, and the like are choices that help manage these risks, while overreliance on frenetic suppliers increases the risk of program and mission failure.

Within the categories of risk, program managers have the ability to provide benefits through careful asset management and decision-making or to increase the likelihood of harm that results from overlooked, unanticipated, or unavoidable developments. Hence, for each of the dimensions of risk, program managers can assess the benefits and possible harms of their decisions about critical assets. We depict this in the matrix in Table 4.1.

Table 4.1 arrays the categories of risk against foreseeable benefits derived from proper IP asset management and potential harms from mismanagement or disregard to IP matters. Looking more closely at reputational risk through IP management, we have tried to capture the sense that IP assets are public creations—meaning that they exist as a special class of assets created through public laws that protect copyrights, patents, and trademarks. The public nature of these assets means that program managers can leverage IP assets to enhance an institution's reputation. In contrast, disregarding the function of IP assets can result in derogatory effects to organizational reputation from legal conflicts.

For example, an agency might adopt a policy that agency-produced IP (such as that developed at a national laboratory or as the product of contractor-enabled software) will be made available to the public to enhance knowledge and innovation or to spur economic growth. The National Aeronautics and Space Administration (NASA) is a prime example of a government agency that actively manages its IP with the goal of achieving the maximum practicable dissemination of the knowledge and IP products it produces.[4] Our interviews with NASA officials indicated that IP management practices are guided

---

[4]   Interview with personnel from the NASA Technology Transfer Program, February 7, 2019.

Table 4.1
Intellectual Property Risk Categories and Related Benefits and Harms

	Reputational Risk	Operational Risk	Credibility Risk	Innovation Risk	Financial or Litigation Risk
Notional benefit	Increased trust, partnership opportunities, and economic growth	Agile acquisition, innovation, and resilient supply chains	Effective messaging, trust in target populations, and reputational defenses	Flexible and agile processes, timely and accurate data, and a culture of forward thinking	Avoidance of legal and financial losses
Notional harm	Embarrassment, legal risk, financial penalties, and forgone partnerships	Procurement disruptions, increased costs, and lack of personnel	Decreased effectiveness, suspicion, and misappropriation of logos and marks	Sole-source contracts, increased costs, and risk aversion in processes and personnel	Legal judgments and loss of resources in time and personnel

principally by the drive to share new knowledge with the world in an attempt to celebrate and support the advancement of science. As a result, NASA licenses its technologies with academic and commercial entities when there are no concerns about export control or security risk. It also maintains a publicly available library of software code (see, for example, Technology Transfer Program, undated). Although it is not inherently part of DHS core missions, public dissemination can offer more holistic benefits to existing programs. Strengthening a program reputation by engaging in public dissemination of IP could give program managers an advantage in other areas.

On the other hand, mismanagement of IP can have deleterious effects on institutional reputations. The primary risk is found in the misappropriation of third-party IP rights, often in the form of patent or copyright infringement. As discussed in Chapter Two, the government has waived its sovereign immunity from copyright- and patent-infringement suits and can be held financially liable for those infractions. Although the direct financial and litigation risks are incorporated in our fifth category of risk, there are additional ramifications in the reputational harms that accrue to agencies or divisions that run afoul of the IP laws. Moreover, because CBP and ICE have statutory authority to protect the United States from counterfeit and IP-infringing products from abroad (such as knock-off handbags and pharmaceuticals), any degree of noncompliance with laws they are purportedly enforcing would be an embarrassment to the department. Thus, DHS program managers have a reputation-based incentive to learn about, resource, and incorporate IP staff support into the decisionmaking and operational processes.

Operational risks are those that frustrate direct progress toward program or mission success through disruptions to processes (or elements of the process, such as staffing and supply chains). A well-managed IP program can be an asset to operational successes by including IP dimensions in the operational planning process and in the execution. We believe that IP support assists in development of more-sophisticated acquisition and procurement processes, particularly in instances in which the department is acquiring third-party support. Procurement risk—which we consider an element of operational risk—

is likely to be of increasing importance as agencies rely more heavily on technologically sophisticated tools for tracking, monitoring, controlling, and advancing the business of national security. In a well-managed program, IP expertise is involved in identifying the needed permissions (both present and expected) for acquisition, sustainment, and maintenance of supplies and materiel. Effective integration, however, would require IP support not only in the contracting process but also in the planning phases. As components grow increasingly reliant on innovative programs and technological sophistication for achieving mission success, this degree of IP integration will become more critical. The limited number of department staff with expertise in IP matters is itself an operational risk that can frustrate the timely response to supporting overall IP management needs. As IP gains greater visibility and recognition, the increased demand will continue to stress the current IP corps unless additional staffing levels are authorized and additional IP talent hired.

Credibility risks are those related to the trustworthiness of the messaging that agencies send out to the general public. At first glance, this area might not seem to be directly related to IP strategy and management. However, the government runs the risk of outside parties trying to trade on its authority and reputation; often, these outside parties will appropriate government messages, symbols, slogans, and logos to attempt to sell products or services that falsely bear the imprimatur of officially sanctioned activities. Although these outside activities are questionable (often illegal) in their own right, the effect on the official programming can be damaging. Trademarks are, in particular, a vitally important part of an effective government messaging strategy when programs need to make their services and initiatives known to target populations. Trademark law is designed to protect the reputation of the original program operators or producers and prevent confusion. Hence, when done correctly, trademarking government programs (we provide some examples below) can help market and communicate needed products and services to target populations. However, the lack of a trademark strategy or the lack of enforcement of a trademark from malicious copycats and hucksters can erode public trust in the official program—even when the official program is delivering on all of its promises. Messages get confused, logos that look suspiciously similar to official government marks intentionally mislead consumers, and program goals are put at risk.

Innovation risks are found where the government's ability to improve, deploy creative new solutions to existing problems, or solve new problems is threatened by a lack of attention to or an insufficient support for IP matters. We believe that an innovative program can leverage IP support to use existing data, tools, and capabilities (often acquired from outside contractor support) to identify new mechanisms for services, such as financial management and human resource tracking, and potentially design "smart" infrastructure at the national borders. In the past, DHS procurement contracts have failed to secure the necessary data and technical rights from their support contractors. This omission—brought about by limited forecasting for needed data in the maintenance and long-term support stages for critical systems—often locks the government into single-source support contracts with firms that retain the data and specifications as trade secrets. This prevents the needed flexibility for innovation, improvements, and efficiency gains, often for many years after the original contract was designed and signed. IP staff can help take a longer-term view by articulating the value, needs, and business case for acquiring data rights up front or later at the government's option. But they can provide this support only if they are included in the procurement process.

Finally, the most obvious risk category related to IP matters is the risk of litigation and financial penalty. This occurs when the government does not abide by IP law and takes actions using other parties' IP without going through the proper channels for licensing, reproduction, acquisition, or partnership. The litigation and financial risks often trigger some of the other harms discussed in conjunction with other risks, such as reputational harms, credibility issues, and loss of innovation partners. Litigation issues present a specific risk because errors in the process results in wasteful consumption of department and component resources. Patent litigation is a protracted process, and, although DOJ is involved, the implicated programs and DHS leadership will have to spend time and effort managing the lawsuits and building back from the associated harms. In these situations, IP staff are a mission requirement for ensuring the prompt and optimal resolution of conflicts. However, the value of IP staff ought to be found in deploying them as a means of preventing and mitigating litigation issues, rather than simply troubleshooting these situations as they arise.

Before moving on to our examples of IP successes and challenges, we additionally note that, within DHS, S&T faces similar risks in carrying out its research, development, and dissemination functions. S&T has the added responsibility, as the R&D arm for DHS, to transition technologies to components. Technology transfer is inherently about managing IP—the creation or acquisition of the ideas and technologies. In doing its work, S&T will either implicitly or explicitly manage IP assets. If it does this well, S&T IP management can secure the technologies that the components need to protect the United States. If it does not, technology transfer can fail to acquire, protect, or transfer the necessary rights to use, share, and reengineer innovative technologies. These possibilities carry similar risks to those outlined above. S&T's reputation is tied to the ability to both develop and deliver technologies. Failure to secure IP rights in acquisition settings can risk the operational successes of programs that rely on those technologies. A series of failures can erode S&T's credibility, both with component end users and with innovation partners in industry. And poor IP management can threaten congressional support, both for S&T programming and for resourcing overall.

We created our notional risk category framework to help demonstrate how IP matters. When effectively managed and included in program decisionmaking, IP resources can reduce many of the risks that DHS and component managers would likely face. We understand that every program faces unique risks and that, consequently, IP is not always a candidate for risk managers' attention. Our intended point is that IP assets are likely to be overlooked unless program managers possess an understanding of the ways in which IP support can enhance the likelihood of success. With the framework provided, managers can begin to explore how IP can help them meet program goals and advance mission success. In the next section, we move from this notional framework to discuss instances in which IP matters have aided and frustrated program goals.

Intellectual Property Vignettes: Successes and Challenges

In this section, we assess the actions and decisions of several subordinate DHS agencies in instances in which efforts regarding IP management have succeeded, as well as examples of situations with added challenges. After reviewing and analyzing our interviews with personnel from the nine subordinate agencies, we selected the following vignettes to serve as representative examples from across the department. We selected CBP, ICE, TSA, and USCIS. We made these selections based on the level of detail provided to the HSOAC interviewers, as well as the applicability of the examples to the core areas of IP (e.g., patent, trademark, procurement, copyright). The vignettes describe instances in which DHS IP staff worked to resolve a particular IP-related concern or incident. We noted that increased resources for IP management purposes might have mitigated or prevented the difficulties that these agencies encountered. In Chapter Five, we provide recommendations for possible mitigation strategies and actions.

We evaluated whether the vignette constituted a success or challenge based on analysis of factors under the five categories of risk: reputational, operational, financial and litigation, credibility, and innovation. We identified these five categories during our interviews with DHS personnel, although we did not necessarily designate them as such. Thus, the categories represent the areas of risk that personnel consistently articulated during discussions, even if they did not specifically refer to them using one of these five terms.

Transportation Security Administration
Success

Many of TSA's systems for aircraft, cargo, and personnel management require the use of new and robust algorithms. Historically, TSA has foraged the market for original equipment manufacturers (OEMs) or similar vendors that can provide devices and algorithms that meet TSA requirements. The drawback to this strategy, however, is that these OEMs inextricably link their respective proprietary detection algorithmic software to the equipment itself. This results in a vendor lock of the IP, with TSA unable to obtain necessary ownership rights. Thus, the current approach then ties TSA to what eventually becomes outdated legacy detection software (and the vendor agreement to which they are tied). This approach has also resulted in significant life-cycle costs that would have been avoided if DHS or TSA developed the IP itself or opted to purchase the IP rights.

In 2018, after close coordination between the DHS and TSA IP legal teams, DHS IP staff implemented a new approach to develop new detection software with broad licensing authorities pursuant to the America Creating Opportunities to Meaningfully Promote Excellence in Technology, Education, and Science (COMPETES) Act (Pub. L. 110-69, 2007).[5] Under this authority, TSA leadership worked with DHS and TSA IP attorneys and staff to develop a national competition for producing an algorithm to accelerate airport passenger screening without compromising safety. The award for the winning algorithm was $1.5 million, and a clause in the award ensured unencumbered DHS/TSA rights of the algorithm and the underlying IP material.[6] This approach presents TSA clear benefits notwithstanding some added challenges. The clear benefit is that TSA is free to self-innovate and generate cutting-edge detection software at reduced cost. That said, challenges remain where, in this particular algorithm example, the agency must still validate a matrix of interchangeable detection software and equipment as meeting TSA requirements. Additionally, prize award efforts by way of the America COMPETES Act generate an increased workload for both TPLD and TSA IP attorney teams because these processes are legally complex.

Notwithstanding the challenges, this approach to obtaining new and valuable IP can significantly reduce three of the five types of risk: operational, financial and litigation, and innovation. In particular,

---

[5] The America COMPETES Act become law in 2007 and was reauthorized in 2011. It includes a provision for federal agencies, such as TSA, to conduct prize competitions for the purposes of spurring innovation to solve current and difficult science, technology, engineering, and mathematics problems that the agency faces. See Public Law 111-358, Section 105. This law provided a means to alleviate aspects of the Bayh–Dole Act of 1980 (35 U.S.C. 206; 37 C.F.R. Part 401), which allows small businesses and other entities to maintain ownership of IP produced using federal funds.

[6] Interview with TSA officials familiar with IP topics, November 13, 2018.

the algorithm will directly affect TSA's ability to screen and process passengers at airports by optimizing passenger and luggage clearance while reducing false positives for threat items (Corrigan, 2018). By essentially purchasing both the algorithm and the underlying IP, TSA will also reduce any subsequent financial and litigation risks. Furthermore, the generation of new IP with the awarding of prize money and with increased rights for TSA (if practical) could mitigate against TSA having to continue to pay for access and use rights or added life-cycle costs associated with a third-party vender owner of the IP. Additionally, because there is no contractual obligation (beyond the $1.5 million payment), TSA will significantly reduce its litigation exposure and risk. Finally, through the competition, TSA will be able to innovate with respect to its current airport security systems, potentially reducing the risk that stale technology will allow security threats to go undetected.

U.S. Citizenship and Immigration Services
Success

USCIS maintains five trademarks (*E-Verify, myE-Verify, ELIS* [the abbreviation for *Electronic Immigration System*], *myUSCIS*, and *SAVE* [the abbreviation for *Systematic Alien Verification for Entitlements*]) for systems that it uses to adjudicate the various types of applications that it receives. Additionally, the agency communicates with millions of employers, citizens, stakeholders, other government agencies, and immigrants each year using both paper and electronic copies of the DHS seal. Immigrants and other categories of applicants have come to trust and rely on these marks and the seal; they indicate that the applicants are communicating with a trusted government agency that exercises real jurisdiction over their status, or the status of a family member, employee, or client, in the United States. The DHS seal is currently without legal protection either as a trademarked item or by a specific statute.[7]

---

[7] In contrast, some component seals are protected from free use by specific statutory provisions. For example, the U.S. Coast Guard seal is protected under 14 U.S.C. 638. As part of an enhanced IP program, it would likely aid both TPLD and agency IP counsel if the DHS seal had statutory protection against free use. This would provide additional authorities not only for cease-and-desist letters but also for enforcement litigation for cases in which DHS or

USCIS officials told us that, to give the impression of being a government operator, an unscrupulous person or company can attempt to take advantage of these populations by misappropriating these marks or the DHS seal. Some of these bad actors engage in immigration benefit fraud, jeopardizing the immigration status and financial well-being of their victims. In response to this, IP counsel for USCIS works with USCIS operators in the field to spot and investigate these illicit uses of the service's marks and the DHS seal. The USCIS attorney then drafts and issues cease-and-desist letters to the offenders to prevent further violations. Because the seal is not specifically protected by law, USCIS relies on both immigration and common-law provisions related to misrepresentation of services. These actions have been successful, albeit limited by the fact that the USCIS attorney we interviewed is the only attorney assigned to IP and 90 percent of the attorney's official time is taken up by other duties.

These efforts have reduced three types of risk for USCIS: operational, credibility, and financial and litigation. For example, by policing the use of its *E-Verify* mark through cease-and-desist letters, USCIS is able to protect employers who rely on the legitimate service in order to check whether their employees have the appropriate immigration status in order to work lawfully in the United States. This serves USCIS's operational mission to ensure the integrity of U.S. immigration laws that relate to work authorization. Preserving *E-Verify* also protects USCIS's reputation as a source for the employee vetting information on which U.S. employers rely.

With regard to policing use of the DHS seal (to the extent possible without enhanced legal protection for the seal), USCIS can reduce operational and financial and litigation risk by reducing the number of bad actors seeking to take advantage of immigrants financially when they apply for legal status. The cease-and-desist letters increase the integrity of the legitimate immigration benefit processes and procedures. When immigrants receive assistance from qualified practitioners to prepare their applications, USCIS adjudicators will more likely have

---

the component feels that such action is necessary to reduce or combat fraudulent use of the seal.

the appropriate information and evidence they need in order to make a decision in accordance with the law, reducing the need for costly investigations or litigation. Additionally, reducing the activity of bad actors lowers adverse credibility risk for USCIS in that it will likely increase the confidence that immigrants will have when communicating with USCIS personnel. Moreover, bad actors that fleece immigrants of their immigration benefit application fees are potentially denying USCIS the ability to capture those fees. Finally, the use of cease-and-desist letters can help USCIS avoid costly affirmative litigation as a means of shutting down organizations that engage in the misappropriation of its trademarks.

Challenge

For many years, USCIS played a video at naturalization ceremonies across the country.[8] Part of the soundtrack of the video included the song "God Bless the USA" by Lee Greenwood. Once, Greenwood was performing at a location where a naturalization ceremony had also occurred. One of Greenwood's staff noticed that USCIS was using Greenwood's copyrighted material and discovered later that USCIS had not obtained usage rights. The agency had to engage in settlement negotiations based on its many years of copyright infringement. This infringement was unintentional. When the video was first created, no IP attorney or qualified individual reviewed it. Furthermore, it remains unclear whether USCIS retained anyone with IP expertise assigned to the agency when the video was created.

The inability to properly review public materials, such as videos, or other information that USCIS might distribute to immigrants and immigration stakeholders affects at least two types of risk: reputational and financial and litigation. Copyright infringement of the type involving Greenwood's IP and for such a lengthy period of time is embarrassing and can be damaging for the agency's public image. The fact that one of DHS's key missions, through ICE, is to investigate and prosecute the theft of IP only exacerbates these adverse impacts (see ICE, 2018b). Additionally, copyright infringement brings the effects

---

[8] USCIS naturalizes approximately nearly 2,000 people daily. See USCIS, 2018b.

of financial risks through settlement actions, enforcement actions, and the costly litigation that can be brought against an agency in violation.

U.S. Immigration and Customs Enforcement
Success

The Homeland Security Investigations (HSI) Forensic Laboratory is one of the many offices supporting ICE operations. The lab provides a broad range of core forensic, intelligence, and investigative support functions to ICE law enforcement agents and staff. These critical services include such capabilities as latent print analysis; fraudulent document examination; training and intelligence information products; polygraph support; and other evidence collection, preservation, and analysis services (USCIS, 2018a). Scientists at the forensic lab frequently devise new methods, approaches, and systems as they perform their duties. Recently, with proactive support from ICE IP counsel and TLPD, ICE has been able to submit a few new patent applications per year.[9]

The efforts to expand the laboratory's patent program affect three key types of risk: operational, financial and litigation, and innovation. First, the opportunity to patent its own methods, systems, and so forth will enable the lab to quickly respond to ICE's operational needs without having to contract with outside vendors. Because ICE has been sued for lab-related patent infringements in the past,[10] holding its own patents will reduce both financial and litigation risks. Additionally, ICE could find itself in a position to license the lab's patented ideas to outside security entities, thereby creating a potential source of revenue for DHS. Last, the ability to patent its own ideas is likely to provide incentives to lab employees to maintain (or increase) their efforts toward developing new, creative, and innovated forensic tools.

Challenge

Prior to becoming part of DHS, ICE responsibilities were part of the legacy U.S. Immigration and Naturalization Service (INS) within

---

[9] Interview with an ICE official familiar with IP topics, November 8, 2018.

[10] Interview with an ICE official familiar with IP topics, November 8, 2018.

DOJ (ICE, 2019). During this time, INS entered into many contracts that placed IP rights in the hands of vendors. Many of these contracts are still in force and have subjected ICE to conditions that prevent it from recompeting the contracts. One example is found on the contract that ICE uses to manage its financial system. ICE has been unable to modernize how it processes many of its financial transactions because a legacy contract has bound the agency to a sole-source provider. This inability to change IP aspects of the current system has prevented ICE from initiating new financial programs.[11] This example shows the far-reaching and long-standing effects of the procurement, acquisition, and contracting of resources where IP review of the documentation might not have properly considered long-term needs.

The long-standing aspects of contractual conditions affecting IP directly corresponds to three of our established risk areas: operational, financial and litigation, and innovation. Operationally, ICE has been impeded from modernizing its financial transactions systems, which affects the ability of personnel to do their jobs efficiently. In terms of financial risk, ICE continues to be beholden to a single-source vendor that might be charging fees at a level that is not cost-effective for ICE and might not represent the most-optimal use of taxpayer funds. Additionally, ICE is unable to recompete this particular contract for fear of the risk of costly federal litigation that could still result in a negative decision. Finally, although ICE has developed many initiatives to modernize its financial system, the contract limits implementation, increasing the risk of failure of the system due to a lack of innovation and development.

U.S. Customs and Border Protection
Success

CBP is one of the components that retains dedicated and specially trained IP staff, actively incorporating IP support into broader agency initiatives to improve mission success, innovation, and planning. Although the IP program at CBP is a little more than one year old, it has engaged in agency-wide conversations about innovation via an

---

[11] Interview with an ICE official familiar with IP topics, November 8, 2018.

innovation initiative that is supported by the CBP commissioner. Despite the fact that much of CBP's technology needs are acquired through commercial off-the-shelf mechanisms, the innovation initiative is broadly assessing the current and future needs of the agency—and has included an IP support function from its early stages.[12]

CBP has three attorneys (the most of any component and second among all entities in DHS and its components only to OGC/IP) who are tasked primarily with working on IP matters.[13] This makes staff more readily available to engage in strategic planning and innovation activities. We believe that these efforts help reduce two types of risk for CBP: reputational and innovation risks (although the CBP staff are engaged in other activities unrelated to the innovation initiative that help to mitigate credibility, operational, and litigation and financial risk as well). The early involvement of IP attorneys in the innovation initiative has helped solve the informational and visibility challenges that this report is intended to highlight. Early-stage engagement mitigates risks and can position the agency to take advantage of the flexibility and agility that innovation provides. The reputational advantages of being an innovative agency builds trust and unlocks a potential new slate of outside firms that will be motivated to partner on new programs and technology.

Challenge
CBP has justified its expansion of the IP program in part because of instances in which IP support was overlooked in the past. CBP has faced patent-infringement litigation in recent years related to optical passport scanning, initiated trademark offensives to protect its CTPAT program from trademark misappropriation by third parties, and has struggled with the technological data and IP dimensions of "smart" border wall acquisition and design.

One anecdote, however, demonstrates how relatively easy it is for program-level managers to overlook IP management, even when the best intentions are motivating their actions. CBP runs a Missing

---

[12] Interview with a CBP official familiar with IP topics.

[13] Interview with a CBP official familiar with IP topics.

Migrant Program (MMP), a humanitarian effort designed to connect undocumented border crossers with emergency medical attention (see CBP, 2018). The program places signage near the border where migrants are known to lose their way. These notifications have location identifiers and instruct migrants to use mobile devices to seek medical and other emergency attention. The responders are not border enforcement officials but humanitarian assistance personnel working with local 911 dispatchers.[14]

However, in an attempt to convey its humanitarian purpose, the program erroneously used the red cross symbol. This image is trademarked and owned by the International Committee of the Red Cross (ICRC) (ICRC, undated). The committee is, by the terms of the Geneva Conventions, the exclusive manager and licenser of the image. International law forbids any use without express permission. CBP received notification from the committee about its usage of the red cross symbol.[15] CBP continues to adapt the program, but the incident reveals how pervasive IP matters remain in DHS operations.

Summary

IP policies and the staff who work on IP issues are assets that the department can deploy to advance mission success. The risk management framework we have presented is designed to help program managers conceptualize the different areas of programmatic risk that are vulnerable without IP resources. In contrast, we have offered vignettes to highlight scenarios in which the department has obtained the unique benefits of expanded IP efforts. Coupled with this notional framework, the representative stories of successes and challenges reveal how IP continually intersects with the work of the department and components on a daily basis. The point of these vignettes is to inform DHS staff—in

---

[14] Interview with a CBP official familiar with IP topics, between October 2018 and May 2019.

[15] Interview with a CBP official familiar with IP topics, between October 2018 and May 2019.

particular, nonattorneys and those without significant IP expertise—of the ways different types of IP are currently incorporated into DHS work. This work can recognize IP as an asset and anticipate the ways in which increased attention to IP can improve mission success, or it can ignore IP and expose programs to mission risk. Given the limited number of staff who have explicit responsibility for IP at the components, IP is likely going unnoticed and unmanaged. That suggests that there are benefits to be reaped by greater inclusion of IP into department and component processes.

In Chapter Five, we sum up our research on the state of DHS IP activities and the opportunities that are currently available and provide some considerations for developing a closer connection between IP and the missions of DHS.

Considerations for Future Management of Intellectual Property

In this report, we have tried to highlight the connection between DHS and component mission areas and the underlying reliance on IP. As government programs invest in developing technology, the department knows that it is likely to find itself increasingly reliant on many dimensions of IP explicitly related to technology. However, technology and IP are not synonymous. A broader range of IP types and the related needs for managing, deploying, and protecting those types will continue to be part of department activities.

In this conclusion, we review our approach and lay out a series of considerations for how DHS might better incorporate IP functionality to greater effect. We provide a set of observations, considerations, and recommendations for advancing the IP program.

A Review of the Study Approach and Core Observations

Tasked with exploring DHS's current approach to managing IP, HSOAC researchers conducted a scan of the types of IP with which the department regularly engages, investigated the management authorities and organizational structures for conducting IP-related work, and performed a gap analysis to find out what is being well managed and what areas might be better addressed through additional resourcing and better management. We spoke with IP staff at the department and component levels, learned the mission areas and were introduced to many of the program-level needs of the components, and concluded that IP has direct connections to mission success and could be better deployed in meeting those goals.

Our research into IP activities at DHS revealed that various dimensions of IP are involved in every component. In other words, all components, and even the work of DHS overall, are intrinsically engaged in regular production, acquisition, and deployment of IP. But despite the universality of IP-related operations, the scope, level of reliance on IP, types of IP, and needed level of professional IP support varied significantly from component to component. In all cases we examined, IP is currently managed as a support function, rather than a direct element of mission risk management (as discussed in the introduction to the framework in Chapter Four).

We found that IP is often an overlooked asset but could be deployed in operational and strategic planning and execution. We recommend that the department reevaluate current methods of incorporating IP programming into departmental resourcing, structure, and strategic planning processes. Furthermore, given that IP is not an area that program managers at DHS routinely consider, we documented five key areas of risk in which IP assets might provide mission-related benefits. This report has explained IP as an important class of mission resources and articulated the need for a more visible role at DHS.

Considerations and Recommendations for Advancing the Intellectual Property Program

To better leverage existing IP assets, DHS will need to consider a series of options for restructuring DHS and component authorities in relation to the following activities: tracking, sharing, and monitoring IP in its possession; funding IP-related activities; and training IP and non-IP staff on the IP assets that the department and components should more actively manage.

Considerations for Structuring Intellectual Property Authorities
The federated structure of decisionmaking at DHS and the components is a result of DHS history and culture—and one that is not likely

to change anytime soon. However, this set of diverse and occasionally contrasting cultures and varied approaches to centralization versus decentralization creates a set of difficulties for monitoring, tracking, and harmonizing IP activities.

As a result, we recommend a DHS-level directive or delegation defining the role between S&T, TPLD, and the components that would delineate roles, responsibilities, and reporting requirements; establish the governance process and procedures for communication, coordination, and reporting; and centralize certain functions with TPLD and decentralize the agency-specific functions to components. We suggest this as a possible breakdown of responsibilities:

- Centralize these functions at TPLD:
  - Prepare and file patent applications.
  - Serve as POC for USPTO (DHS's single voice to USPTO).
  - Manage the ISA program.
  - With support from component counsel, handle all litigation, trademark- and copyright-infringement defense, and affirmative enforcement actions.
  - Manage licensing agreements.
  - Negotiate and manage international agreements and CRADAs.
  - Oversee the invention-disclosure program.
  - Manage and track the ICANN process.
  - Track and monitor the following DHS-wide:
    ○ new R&D
    ○ invention disclosures and inventions
    ○ cease-and-desist letters issued
    ○ DHS patents and licensing agreements
    ○ contracts containing IP clauses
    ○ ISA reviews
    ○ technology and patent foraging results and open-source and free-use IP (for R&D use).
- Delegate these functions to components:
  - Review all procurement, acquisition, and contracts containing IP clauses or conditions, such as
    ○ data rights

- ◦ licensing
- ◦ subscriptions
- ◦ maintenance and development
- ◦ sourcing
- ◦ copyrighted or otherwise protected material.
- – Identify and assist in preparation of patent, trademark, and copyright applications.
- – Conduct trademark and copyright scrapes for enforcement and infringement actions.[1]
- – Monitor licensing agreements.
- – Issue cease-and-desist letters.
- – Report all relevant IP actions to TPLD for tracking and monitoring purposes.
- – Identify, report, and monitor invention disclosures.
- – Identify and conduct initial ISA reviews with component subject-matter experts.
- – Train contracting staff and other personnel involved with IP.

This list is meant to encourage a policy development conversation, rather than be viewed as a definitive recommendation that DHS should adopt. Of course, the responsibilities, functions, and overall level of effort will be tied to the funding levels and mechanisms available to each office.

In short, the current arrangement does not provide strong-enough guidance on structural elements for how the components and TPLD can work together and how the people who perform and oversee the IP functions can better share, evaluate, and strategize their efforts in service to the missions of their respective components and DHS overall.

Considerations for Intellectual Property Knowledge Management

As a foundational matter, DHS should develop a DHS-wide system of sharing information for IP tracking and management. This process should include an accounting of types of IP (including such knowl-

---

[1]   *Web scrape* refers to systematized, investigative internet searches for particular content, such as key words.

edge products as patents, trademarks, invention disclosures, data resources, and open-source repositories), as well as policies, directives, guidance, and training materials. To enable this system, all IP staff will need to input, track, monitor, and update all component-level IP actions, procurements, acquisitions, contracts, trademarks, and training opportunities.

The benefits of such a system would be significant. This model would help reduce duplicative resource purchasing; enable TPLD to input, track, monitor, and deliver information regarding patents, inventions, trademarks, and copyrights to IP personnel DHS-wide; and provide a library of resources and references for common problems that DHS employees come across so that IP attorneys can direct inquiries to those sources. In essence, this is a recommendation for better knowledge-management practices as a way of supporting the visibility and usefulness of IP assets. The issues that DHS faces are not questions of the value of managing IP assets but of their visibility across the enterprise.

Knowledge management also includes the regularization of training and education, both for IP attorneys and for the department. DHS should establish a training and knowledge-management group to produce DHS-wide IP training modules for employees, contracting officers, project managers, and other staff who regularly manage IP assets. We recommend a yearly conference for all DHS IP attorneys and staff for training, education, knowledge, network strengthening, and awareness. And a special education effort should be required to apprise higher-level managers of IP's strategic and planning-level benefits to the department and the components. Without top-level support, IP is likely to remain a back-office function and, therefore, underutilized as a mission asset.

Considerations for Funding Intellectual Property–Related Activities

The major hurdle facing a more robust IP program at the department and components is found in resource requirements. IP functionality is supported by a very small cadre of IP professionals who have the specialized training, knowledge, and expertise to leverage DHS and component assets in direct, mission-relevant ways. Those staff are providing support to their programs, but they are underfunded given both the current demands on their time and the opportunities for more-effective and -powerful uses of IP assets in service to the mission. For example, although responding to patent-infringement litigation is an essential IP role, components ought to consider bolstering IP staffing levels so that other IP-related functions are performed when there is a surge in litigation-related work.

At the moment, staffing levels only allow an either/or approach to IP work, although we recommend staffing levels that allow a both/and approach. IP staff should be able to scale efforts to surges in litigation needs and continue to perform the other IP asset management functions that we describe in this report. In our estimation, no component has adequately reached this level of resourcing. Furthermore, some components have no dedicated, specially trained IP staff at all. Although this is perhaps an appropriate situation and staffing determination for smaller agencies (FLETC handles relatively little IP material, for example), some core IP functions related to procurement, contract review, invention disclosure, and litigation risk are not being adequately monitored. This suggests having a minimum of one IP attorney at each component beyond current staffing levels. Of course, as IP is better managed, opportunities and additional IP assets will be discovered, new training needs will be revealed, and IP will be integrated as a strategic asset in operational decisionmaking, and those will all drive requirements for additional IP-fluent attorneys.

Establishing the appropriate staffing levels with any specificity is impossible at this time, given the needed structural decisions (and their implications on staffing) and the imminent push into ISA reviews. Indeed, conversations with DHS and component managers revealed that they might need to seek permission for DHS to move from the general-schedule salary scale to a pay-banding scale that will enable the office to hire and retain a cadre of experienced IP attorneys. Recruitment and retention for highly skilled and much-in-demand IP attorneys will be a challenge at current salary levels.

Overall, as DHS tries to determine the resourcing levels for its IP function, it will need to answer the following questions:

- What IP functions are to be performed by component attorneys, and what functions will be performed by TPLD staff?
- Once the functional division is settled, what level of effort will be required to meet component- and department-level demand?
- Where are there current backlogs of IP work, and what staffing levels would clear the need?
- What is the level of *unknown demand*, including
  - the number of currently unfiled invention disclosures (from both government employees and contractors)
  - the number of potential patent filings from invention disclosures
  - the number of untrademarked logos for component-sponsored public programs
  - the number of contracts for software and data rights that should have IP consultation as a matter of course?

We call this last category *unknown demand* because the lack of component-level IP staff has produced a blind spot for the resourcing calculus. A component knows that it needs attorney support when it is served with a lawsuit for patent infringement. However, the more difficult estimating question concerns the latent need that will be revealed only once DHS surveys the program offices about how they could utilize additional IP support and consults leadership about how it could use IP advice and guidance in strategic planning.

Conclusion

In this report, we have evaluated whether there is a connection between IP activities and mission support, identified some ways in which IP can support the mission (through risk management), and provided evidence that current levels of IP support are insufficient to meet all of the current need. DHS is a department founded to protect national security but is underutilizing an asset that can be deployed in that fight. As the technological sophistication of both the U.S. government and its adversaries advances at a rapid pace, IP concerns, threats, and opportunities are likely to increase in number, scope, and sophistication. An assessment and decision on the right structure, level of support, and integration of the IP function into DHS decisionmaking are warranted.

Department of Homeland Security Components' Intellectual Property Practices

In this appendix, we expand on and extend Chapter Three's discussion of the IP practices of DHS subordinate components and relate those practices to the components' goals, missions, priorities, and/or objectives.

U.S. Citizenship and Immigration Services

Overview and Mission

USCIS is charged with overseeing lawful immigration into the United States, including citizenship and naturalization, family- and employment-based permanent residence, temporary employment authorization, refugee and asylum status, and international adoption. USCIS meets these responsibilities through the vetting and adjudication of applications and petitions for these immigration benefits (USCIS, 2018a). Created in 2003, USCIS assumed the immigration service functions from what was then INS (USCIS, 2011). Currently, USCIS is made up of approximately 19,000 government employees and contractors located in more than 200 offices worldwide (USCIS, undated). The service's mission is to administer "the nation's lawful immigration system, safeguarding its integrity and promise by efficiently and fairly adjudicating requests for immigration benefits while protecting Americans, securing the homeland, and honoring our values" (USCIS, undated).

On a typical day, USCIS adjudicates more than 26,000 requests for immigration benefits, naturalizes nearly 2,000 new citizens, grants lawful residence (i.e., "green card" status) to approximately 2,100 people, and verifies the employment eligibility of more than 80,000 new hires in the United States (USCIS, 2018b). USCIS is headed by a director and deputy director and consists of seven operational directorates: External Affairs; Field Operations; Fraud Detection and National Security; Immigration Records and Identity Services; Management; Refugee, Asylum, and International Operations; and Service Center Operations. Each is headed by an associate director (USCIS, 2010). Figure A.1 shows an organizational chart.

In its strategic plan, USCIS outlines five goals, each with several corresponding objectives for the service to meet in order to achieve it (USCIS, 2016):

- Goal 1: Identify, address, and mitigate national security and fraud risks to the immigration system.
  - Objective 1.1: Enhance understanding and collaboration across USCIS about national security and fraud risk management.
  - Objective 1.2: Strengthen intergovernmental sharing and use of information to minimize national security risks and facilitate effective case processing.
  - Objective 1.3: Advance a more comprehensive and systematic approach to detection and mitigation of fraud risks across the immigration system.
- Goal 2: Deliver consistently high-quality services.
  - Objective 2.1: Continue to build a shared culture of equality.
  - Objective 2.2: Deliver clear and timely guidance.
  - Objective 2.3: Strengthen the flexibility of USCIS service delivery.
  - Objective 2.4: Strengthen program management, acquisition management, and financial management.
- Goal 3: Enable the USCIS workforce to excel in a dynamic environment.
  - Objective 3.1: Promote a shared understanding of the meaning and importance of the USCIS mission.
  - Objective 3.2: Develop agency leaders to shape and lead an evolving organization.

Figure A.1
U.S. Citizenship and Immigration Services Organizational Chart

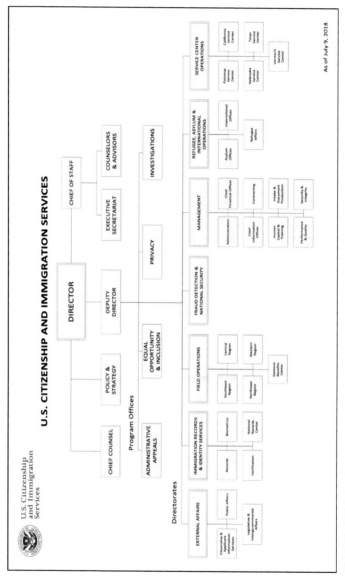

SOURCE: USCIS, 2018c.

- – Objective 3.3: Develop a workforce prepared to address chang-
  ing needs.
- • Goal 4: Promote the importance, rights, and responsibilities of
  citizenship.
  - – Objective 4.1: Increase immigrants' understanding of civics,
    citizenship, and the naturalization process.
  - – Objective 4.2: Highlight the importance of citizenship to
    immigrants and the nation.
- • Goal 5: Enhance USCIS interactions with customers, stakehold-
  ers, and the general public.
  - – Objective 5.1: Strengthen USCIS's understanding of customer
    and stakeholder needs.
  - – Objective 5.2: Provide an enhanced experience across all cus-
    tomer and stakeholder interactions.

Many of USCIS's goals and related objectives have an IP dimension that can facilitate increased operational success. In general, USCIS
relies heavily on software and technology to process and adjudicate
applications for admission into the United States. The capability to
address IP aspects related to these functions is crucial for USCIS to
conduct operations in a manner that is innovative, agile, secure, and
fiscally responsible.

We base the descriptions in the rest of this section on information gleaned during an interview with USCIS officials familiar with IP
topics on November 14, 2018.

Current Intellectual Property Portfolio, Staffing, and Needs

Most IP concerns for USCIS relate to its acquisition and use of software
and technology, with additional issues related to trademarks, patents,
and licensing issues. As USCIS continues to move toward digitization
and processing of all immigration-related forms, applications, and petitions (B. Johnson, 2018; see also USCIS, 2016, p. 6, note 8), these IP
concerns will likely increase. Moreover, as USCIS seeks to expand its
engagement in the digital sphere with not only applicants and petition-
ers but also those who are granted some form of immigration status,
private entities, and the general public, IP monitoring and management

will likely become important and more resource intensive. Currently, IP matters are handled by a sole attorney within the USCIS Office of Chief Counsel's Commercial and Administrative Law Division. This attorney relies heavily on support from TPLD, with IP matters representing about 10 percent of the position's responsibilities. However, this level of effort has been growing as demands with respect to copyright, trademarks, patent litigation, and acquisition-related issues rise.

Copyright
Related Goals and Objectives: 2 (2.2 and 2.3), 3 (3.1, 3.2, and 3.3), 4 (4.1 and 4.2), and 5 (5.2)

As an agency of nearly 20,000 employees and contractors, USCIS conducts an extensive amount of training, both internally and contracted through outside entities. The design, production, and deployment of training materials frequently raise fair-use questions that require analysis and action to ensure that the agency does not violate copyright. Additionally, many naturalization events are public and involve the use of copyrighted, or copyrightable, material. One significant example involved the use of the song "God Bless the USA" by singer/songwriter Lee Greenwood. For many years, USCIS played the song during naturalization ceremonies. When Greenwood's representatives discovered this, they barred USCIS from using the song and forced it to enter into costly settlement negotiations (represented by DOJ) to compensate Greenwood and avoid potentially more costly litigation.

Trademark Registration and Enforcement
Related Goals and Objectives: 1 (1.3), 4 (4.1 and 4.2), and 5 (5.2)

USCIS currently holds five trademarks: *E-Verify*, *myE-Verify*, *ELIS* (the abbreviation for *Electronic Immigration System*), *myUSCIS*, and *SAVE* (the abbreviation for *Systematic Alien Verification for Entitlements*). At this time, USCIS has no organic ability to investigate or conduct web scrapes to determine the violation of its trademarks.[1] The DHS seal itself, when combined with the title "U.S. Citizenship and Immigration Services," is a mark that is frequently misappropriated by those

---

[1]   In this instance, USCIS has no personnel to conduct these searches to determine whether its marks are being misappropriated.

seeking to misrepresent themselves as associated with or approved by the service. Evidence, in the form of several cease-and-desist letters issued by USCIS counsel each year, indicates that USCIS trademark rights are being violated and are at continued risk. We provide two examples to highlight this issue.

First, USCIS field personnel report that physicians authorized by USCIS to serve as civil surgeons for the purposes of conducting immigrant medical examinations have produced materials using the DHS seal in combination with the service's title. The misuse of these marks gives immigrants the false impression that they are interacting with agents of the federal government. Second, field personnel report that people who act as "preparers" of documents for intending immigrants frequently misappropriate the DHS seal and department or service title.[2] In some cases, unscrupulous preparers have used the marks to take advantage of immigrants by charging costly fees for services they are not certified to provide. Additionally, some preparers have falsely claimed to prepare and file documents that are never filed or have filed documents that are inaccurate and damage immigrants' standing before USCIS. In doing so, the misuse of these marks puts the reputation and integrity of the entire immigration benefit system at risk. Overall, USCIS personnel believe that more could be done in terms of detecting instances of violation, producing cease-and-desist orders, and following up on those orders with better tracking and enforcement.

Patent Litigation
Related Goals and Objectives: 1 (1.2 and 1.3), 2 (2.4), and 5 (5.2)
USCIS does not currently have a program for patent acquisition. However, it is frequently the defendant in patent-infringement litigation brought by holders of patents for technology that the service uses. The technology most often at issue relates to card stock (i.e., identification cards to indicate an immigration benefit or status), including card production, radio-frequency identification chips, and card-reading devices. At this writing, USCIS is engaged in four such lawsuits, and

---

[2] *Intending immigrant* refers to a foreign national or foreign-born person who enters the United States with the intention to reside permanently in the United States. See 8 U.S.C. 1101(a)(15).

the amount of related litigation has been increasing. Given the fact that the service produces thousands of cards daily, this is an area of increasing risk and liability.

Acquisition, Procurement, and Contracts
Related Goals and Objectives: 1 (1.3), 4 (4.1 and 4.2), 3 (3.3), and 5 (5.1 and 5.2)

USCIS purchases billions of dollars' worth of software and equipment to meet its goals (see generally Office of Inspector General, 2016). Personnel interviewed on the subject described the service as a "power buyer" for software. This level of demand has left current staff unable to fully review all procurement and acquisition contracts for appropriate IP-related language and protections. Many of USCIS's software purchases fall in the "micro" category, defined as transactions for less than $5 million. Therefore, an attorney reviews the documentation and contracts associated with these procurements for IP conditions and languages only if the contracting officer deems it necessary. USCIS lacks the resources to establish a system of IP document review for all software purchases. This puts the agency at risk with respect to data-rights ownership, modifications, and maintenance. USCIS could very well be paying more than necessary for these rights and services because IP-knowledgeable staff cannot sufficiently review and edit procurement and acquisition documentation.

Additionally, USCIS does not possess the resources to properly track and account for software licenses and subscriptions, making it vulnerable if a vendor company initiated an audit (which is frequently given as a conditional right to the vendor upon acquisition). Given that USCIS employs thousands of officers who use its various software systems, unintended use in excess of licenses could expose the service to millions of dollars in liability.

Moreover, USCIS lacks the necessary IP staff and cross-organizational access to determine whether other offices or components within DHS have made the same or similar purchase or acquisition. For example, at least three other components (ICE, CBP, and the USCG) regularly interact with people who lack proper immigration status. However, USCIS personnel have no way of identifying potential duplications with respect to IP-related materials that these other organizations might already own (and vice versa). This puts the service at risk for redundant purchase and acquisition of software, systems, or other products that might already be available.

Finally, USCIS might also be at risk of forgoing a valuable licensing opportunity with respect to its E-Verify program. E-Verify is a USCIS-owned database system that allows employers in the United States to verify the immigration status of a potential hire. This allows the employer to verify I-9 information provided by the potential employee and avoid violation of immigration laws that bar hiring people without appropriate immigration status. Employers do not currently pay any fees to USCIS to use and access the E-Verify service.

Organizations that employ large numbers of people have begun to hire firms with tools, such as Oracle and its PeopleSoft software, to confirm large batches of candidates at a time. These firms charge the potential employer a fee to conduct these E-Verify checks, despite the fact that E-Verify is a free service. Because USCIS expends its own funds to operate E-Verify, one IP option for the service to consider would be to license E-Verify to private-sector firms, such as Oracle, that currently profit from this free service. This move would enable the service to recoup the costs associated with developing and maintaining E-Verify and use the licensing fees to finance an expansion of E-Verify, which is one of the service's goals.

Invention Secrecy Act

USCIS does not currently engage in ISA reviews. USCIS's principal mission, to adjudicate immigration benefit petitions and applications, involves fraud-detection methods and technology. However, USCIS personnel indicated during interviews that their fraud measures (mostly related to document veracity) lack unique aspects such that the agency would be concerned about patents related to counterfeiting and document alteration.

U.S. Coast Guard

Overview and Mission

Congress established the USCG, the oldest of the DHS components, in 1790 (1 Stat. Ch. VII). At the time of its founding, the USCG's purpose was to ensure the fidelity of tariffs, enforce trade laws, and prevent smuggling. Until the formation of the Navy in 1798, the USCG served as the nation's only marine force (Historian's Office, undated b). The USCG's mission has continually grown in scope, yet the organization retains the original purpose and intention given by Congress. The USCG's mission is "to ensure our Nation's maritime safety, security, and stewardship" (Historian's Office, undated a). To achieve this mission, the USCG is organized by geographic regions of responsibility, mission support divisions, operational divisions, and direct-report offices to Coast Guard headquarters. Figure A.2 provides the organizational chart for the USCG.

The USCG's *Strategic Plan 2018–2022* (USCG, 2018) does not supply goals but designates the organization's strategic priorities and supporting objectives. The USCG's overall framework is to be "ready, relevant, and responsive." To remain capable in these areas, the USCG pursues three strategic priorities (USCG, 2018, p. 8), along with objectives under each priority:

- Goal 1: Maximize readiness today and tomorrow.
  - Objective 1.1: Cultivate the mission-ready total workforce, which includes providing support programs and skill-development opportunities to help recruit and retain talented people, including those in the ready and auxiliary reserves (USCG, 2018, p. 12).
  - Objective 1.2: Modernize assets, infrastructure, and mission platforms, which includes strengthening and modernizing critical systems and support programs while acquiring necessary assets and technologies to meet future needs and challenges (USCG, 2018, p. 14).

Figure A.2
U.S. Coast Guard Organizational Chart

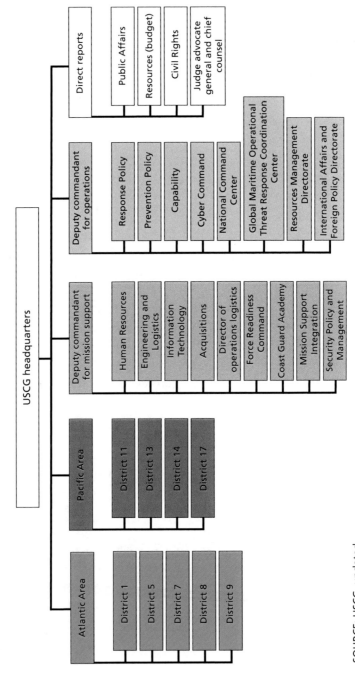

SOURCE: USCG, undated.

- Goal 2: Address the nation's complex maritime challenges.
  - Objective 2.1: Strengthen maritime governance, which includes enhancing situational awareness to protect maritime borders; shaping safe, secure, and environmentally responsible activities across the maritime domain; and provide effective presence through the use of technology and innovation (USCG, 2018, p. 18).
  - Objective 2.2: Enhance unified effort through improved integration with DHS, the utilization of capabilities to support DoD efforts, the cultivation of partnerships with members of the maritime community and building partner-nation capacity through international engagement (USCG, 2018, p. 20).
- Goal 3: Deliver mission excellence anytime, anywhere.
  - Objective 3.1: Strengthen resilience through crisis leadership, emergency preparedness, and surge response. This objective includes being the lead for integrated responses to maritime disasters, planning for crisis and surge incidents, and identifying and using advanced information technology to support crisis efforts (USCG, 2018, p. 24).
  - Objective 3.2: Innovate for better organizational performance, which includes providing mission support as quickly as needed, balancing risk management, demonstrating organizational and decisionmaking agility, and encouraging a culture of innovation within the USCG (USCG, 2018, p. 26).

We collected the information presented in the rest of this section during an interview with USCG officials familiar with IP topics on December 12, 2018.

Current Intellectual Property Portfolio, Staffing, and Needs

The USCG has substantive equities in each of the categories of IP. It also has a broad mission set that includes both maritime national security and law enforcement tasks. This expansive set of missions involves patents, trademarks, copyrights, invention disclosures, procurement and acquisition, and invention-secrecy concerns. Currently, IP matters are handled by a sole attorney within the USCG Office of Judge Advocate General and Chief Counsel's General Law Division. This attorney relies heavily on receiving support from TPLD because IP matters represent approximately 20 to 25 percent of the position's responsibilities. However, the demands for these efforts has been increasing with respect to trademarks, copyrights, and acquisition-related issues.

Trademark Registration and Enforcement
Related Goals and Objectives: 1 (1.1) and 2 (2.1 and 2.2)

The USCG both generates and makes use of a significant amount of material for training, administrative, and operational purposes. The service has struggled to ensure that it properly uses and distributes the copyrighted materials that it contracts. Additionally, the agency has struggled to determine the limits of copyright protection for any given material—that is, which uses are prohibited and which materials are subject to more-open fair-use conditions. Although the service has not yet been subject to instances of copyright-infringement actions, IP counsel believes this to be an area of significant risk, based on the frequency of requests for advice in this area. Additionally, interaction between IP counsel and USCG managers and operators has indicated, anecdotally, a strong need for employee training in this area so that employees can avoid instances of copyright infringement and potentially costly litigation.

The USCG has several trademarks, most using some form of the USCG seal, that are used in advertising, recruiting, and inspection and certification processes. Generally speaking, the USCG seal is protected by federal statute (see 14 U.S.C. 639). Therefore, the service does not have to file copyright applications in most cases involving the use of its seal, and the service's own statutory protections allow it to engage in enforcement actions.

IP counsel at the USCG spends a significant amount of time on trademark-enforcement actions. The USCG's seal is often misappropriated by private organizations that claim to assist prospective applicants who seek to join the USCG. These organizations typically assist with preparing and filing paperwork, determining eligibility requirements, and processing. By misappropriating the seal, these organizations give the false impression to applicants, who might be as young as 17 years old, that they are operating under the supervision of the USCG. IP counsel reports that applicants are often taken advantage of in these situations financially and that, in the worst cases, their recruitment eligibility can be put at risk. Additionally, the USCG provides certification markings for maritime equipment, such as personal flotation devices and other safety devices, upon inspection of such equipment. These certifications can be valuable for the manufacturers of these devices because they lend credibility to the operational effectiveness of the device itself. Misappropriation of these markings in this case can result in consumer deception: Buyers and users are misled to believe that the devices have been sufficiently tested to guarantee a certain durability and safety level.

The USCG takes these trademark violations very seriously. However, because the service has only one IP counsel, its ability to detect infringements and engage in enforcement actions (primarily through the use of cease-and-desist letters) has been impeded. IP counsel for the USCG believes that the service could initiate five to ten additional enforcement actions (either by issuance of a cease-and-desist letter or by bringing a federal court action) per year.

Patent Litigation
Related Goals and Objectives: 1 (1.2), 2 (2.1), and 3 (3.1)

The USCG has not been engaged in any component-specific patent litigation conflicts; however, this historical boon does not indicate service immunity.[3] Currently, the USCG holds two patents. One is for a device for removing a buoy split key; the other is for a quick-release flare tube adapter. Additionally, the USCG has a patent pending on a linear generator for homogeneous charge compression ignition. Furthermore, the service has two inventions developed by USCG personnel or USCG contractors that are covered under DHS invention disclosure guidelines: a CherryMAX extraction tool and a corrosion monitoring system.

IP counsel for the USCG noted that, as patent and invention numbers increase, the risk of patent litigation would increase as well.

---

[3]   USCG is named from time to time in DHS-wide patent lawsuits.

Additionally, the USCG does not have any current resources to perform searches or web scrapes to detect infringements on its current and future patents or on any future inventions that might require protection. Currently, the USCG's General Law Division is not staffed for such an increase and would have to rely almost exclusively on TPLD resources to defend the service in any patent-related matters. Alternatively, either DHS or the USCG should consider creating and funding additional IP positions to absorb the potential increase in workload.

Acquisition, Procurement, and Contracts
Related Goals and Objectives: 1 (1.2), 2 (2.1), and 3 (3.1)
The USCG is a major procurement and contracting organization. It is a force of more than 49,000 service members and personnel (USCG, 2016). The 2017 procurement, construction, improvement, and R&D budget was approximately $1.4 billion (USCG, 2019). Nevertheless, IP counsel reported having insufficient resources to conduct a review of major contracts for IP-related clauses and conditions. The USCG relies on its contracting officers and other contract reviewers (e.g., procurement attorneys, program managers) to ensure general legal and FAR compliance. However, at this time, there is no designated contract review process for IP-specific contracting issues. This presents significant risks for the USCG, particularly with respect to contracts involving data rights, software licensing, and maintenance and development life-cycle costs. IP counsel has indicated a strong need for the USCG to implement an IP review program for USCG contracts.

Additionally, the USCG currently owns IP material (patents and trademarks) for which it already has statutory authority to license to third parties (see 10 U.S.C. 2260). In fact, the USCG has licensed the use of its various trademarks and protected seals but has not had sufficient resources to develop licensing contracts that would allow it to capture a fee. Despite this opportunity to increase service revenue, the USCG does not have the staffing needed for this task.

Invention Secrecy Act
Related Goals and Objectives: 1 (1.2), 2 (2.1), and 3 (3.1)
The USCG is not currently engaged in ISA reviews. However, IP counsel stressed that the service is greatly concerned about future patentable

IP that could hamper, impede, or threaten the service's mission. For example, the USCG is slated (upon receipt of funding) to build several new types of ships in the near future. One type of ship of particular note is a proposed polar icebreaker—specifically, because of the technology involved in designing and producing sections of it (e.g., hull, onboard scientific equipment). The USCG can seek review under the ISA for patents related to these types of technologies and possibly for other maritime technologies related to detection and interdiction.

Countering Weapons of Mass Destruction Office

Overview and Mission

CWMD is a support component of DHS charged with authorities over the following: (1) radiological and nuclear activities; (2) biodefense activities; (3) terrorism risk assessments and material threat assessments; (4) food, agriculture, and veterinary defense; (5) chemical activities; (6) medical and public health; and (7) operations support (DHS, 2018e; Nielsen, 2018). CWMD accomplishes these goals by consolidating key functions and efforts within DHS to prevent the use of chemical, biological, radiological, and nuclear materials in a manner that might be harmful to the United States or its interests. The office is also charged with policy coordination and strategic planning to counter threats of weapons of mass destruction (WMD) (DHS, 2017). CWMD is headed by an assistant secretary and a principal deputy assistant secretary. It consists of four directorates: Enterprise Services; Operations Support; Systems Support; and Policy, Plans, Analysis and Requirements.

CWMD is one of DHS's newest offices. In December 2017, the secretary of DHS announced the office's creation, and she consolidated the following groups under one organization: the Domestic Nuclear Detection Office and a majority of the Office of Health Affairs, as well as elements of the Office of Strategy, Policy, and Plans and the Office of Operations Coordination (DHS, 2018e). The secretary formally granted the office its specifically delegated powers in May 2018 (see Nielsen, 2018). With its passage on December 21, 2018, the Countering Weapons of Mass Destruction Act of 2018 (Pub. L. 115-387) fully established CWMD (DHS, 2018e). The mission of CWMD is to "counter attempts by terrorist or other threat actors to carry out an attack against the United States or its interests using a weapon of mass destruction" (DHS, 2018e).

CWMD has not yet formulated a formal strategic plan. However, the office does have three strategic goals: (1) enhance the nation's abilities to prevent terrorists and other threat actors from using WMD, (2) support operational partners in closing capability gaps along adversary pathways, and (3) invest in and develop innovative technologies to meet partner requirements and improve operations (DHS, 2018e). Notwithstanding a formal strategic plan or guidance document, the secretary of DHS issued a delegation of authority to the assistant secretary of CWMD (see generally Nielsen, 2018). From this document, we have extrapolated the following key goals and objectives:

- Goal 1: Engage in radiological and nuclear activities.
  - Objective 1.1: Develop policies and operation plans for preventing and responding to nuclear and radiological threats.
  - Objective 1.2: Perform science and technology responsibilities, including advising the secretary on R&D.
  - Objective 1.3: Establish priorities for funding, R&D, test and evaluation, and procurement for technology and systems.
  - Objective 1.4: Develop or acquire research and prototypes related to radiological and nuclear detection countermeasures.
- Goal 2: Engage in chemical and biodefense activities.
  - Objective 2.1: Develop policies and plans to prevent threats from biological weapons, global pandemics, and infectious diseases.
  - Objective 2.2: Lead biodefense activities consistent with end-to-end planning for attacks, surveillance integration, and early-warning systems.
  - Objective 2.3: Establish requirements for R&D activities related to biodefense.
  - Objective 2.4: Coordinate the DHS Medical Countermeasures Program.

- Objective 2.5: Develop policies and plans for responding to and preventing chemical weapon threats.
- Objective 2.6: Manage DHS's operational chemical detection programs.
- Goal 3: Conduct terrorism risk assessments and material threat assessments.
  - Objective 3.1: Conduct non-R&D functions related to biological, radiological, nuclear, and chemical terrorism risk assessment (in coordination with other relevant government agencies).
  - Objective 3.2: Coordinate R&D functions related to biological, radiological, nuclear, and chemical risk assessments.
  - Objective 3.3: Coordinate defense for food, agriculture, and veterinary systems against terrorism and other high-consequence events.
- Goal 4: Protect medical programs and public health.
  - Objective 4.1: Oversee DHS operational medical programs (detainee health care, emergency medical activities, and medical personnel assigned to DHS).
  - Objective 4.2: Provide medical direction; approve procurement; and oversee use of controlled substances by DHS components, law enforcement, and laboratory safety programs.
- Goal 5: Provide operational support.
  - Objective 5.1: Support and ensure effective, coordinated medical response to natural or human-caused disasters or acts of terrorism related to chemical, nuclear, biological, or radiological events.
  - Objective 5.2: Support the National Operations Center and National Response Coordination Center with regard to medical support for biological incidents.
  - Objective 5.3: Develop policy and requirements for funding mechanisms for operation medical and public health activities.

Many of CWMD's goals and related objectives have a direct IP dimension that facilitates the achievement of objectives and fulfillment of the particular mission. In general, CWMD relies heavily on technology and systems to detect, prevent, and coordinate radiological, biological, nuclear, and chemical risks, threats, and events. The capability to address IP aspects related to these functions is, and will continue to be, crucial in order for CWMD to conduct its policies, plans, and operations in a manner that is innovative, agile, secure, and fiscally responsible.

We collected the information in the rest of this section during an interview with CWMD officials familiar with IP topics on November 13, 2018.

Current Intellectual Property Portfolio, Staffing, and Needs

Most IP concerns for CWMD relate to acquisition and procurement activities. Presently, the office struggles to ensure that appropriate IP-related clauses are included in contract documentation. Additionally, CWMD is typically the respondent in a few IP-related lawsuits per year, with four or five IP-related suits in the past year. CWMD is also involved in CRADAs (through S&T) and has a small number of copyright and trademark concerns. Given that the office has now been established by statute, it is conceivable that its IP needs will increase, particularly given its extensive purview over R&D.[4]

Currently, CWMD IP matters are handled by two attorneys from OGC. These attorneys rely heavily on support from TPLD. They devote approximately 10 percent of their time to IP-related issues other than litigation. When they are involved in an IP-related lawsuit, however, the associated tasks typically absorb 100 percent of their time. Additionally, both attorneys reported being detailed to other DHS component offices to provide support for IP litigation conflicts. Our interview revealed that these attorneys also provide IP training to staff and contracting officers within CWMD.

---

[4] Statutory designation, as a general matter, enables DHS to more effectively request resources from Congress for an office when it submits its annual budget plan. Increased resources will likely enable CWMD to procure and acquire R&D capabilities, as well as produce more IP on behalf of DHS.

Trademark Registration and Enforcement
Related Goals and Objectives: 1 (1.1, 1.2, 1.3, and 1.4) and 3 (3.1, 3.2, and 3.3)

CWMD operates the Graduated Rad/Nuc Detector Evaluation and Reporting (GRaDER) program. This program is mandated by Congress to set technical capability standards and implement a test and evaluation program for preventive radiological and nuclear detection equipment in the United States. GRaDER evaluates commercial, off-the-shelf radiological and nuclear detection equipment against the national standards required by mission capabilities. Although the program is still in development, *GRaDER* is a protected trademark. Once the program is fully operational, DHS will need to vigilantly protect and defend the mark against potential misuse. An improperly marked device might not meet the technical standards necessary to detect a radiological or nuclear device.

Patent Litigation
Related Goals and Objectives: 1 (1.1 through 1.4), 2 (2.1 through 2.6), and 3 (3.1 through 3.3)

CWMD typically defends itself in four to five patent litigation lawsuits per year. These conflicts are resource-intensive activities and are typically related to CWMD's acquisition and procurement of technology, systems, and software required for threat detection and assessment. These cases are on a strict, docketed timeline that requires the IP attorneys at CWMD to devote 100 percent of their operational time to properly litigate on the office's behalf.

Acquisition, Procurement, and Contracts
Related Goals and Objectives: 1 (1.1 through 1.4), 2 (2.1 through 2.6), and 3 (3.1 through 3.3)

At present, CWMD has a considerable gap with regard to its capability to procure the appropriate data rights associated with its acquisition of software, systems, and technologies. The inability to procure these data rights directly hinders CWMD's ability to perform its missions. For example, vendors typically develop algorithms related to various types of detection equipment and software. Without appropriate data-rights clauses in the contracts, vendors are currently able to prevent

CWMD from accessing important data related to the technology. CWMD is then forced to comply with the vendor's pricing for data or other limiting conditions on its use. Additionally, if the environment in which the detection equipment is placed changes, the algorithm must adapt. Without sufficient contractual rights to request the adaptation, CWMD must abide by the vendor agreement.

Many of the purchases related to the data-rights issues are $500,000 or less in value. Currently, these micro purchases do not require a full review by an IP attorney with respect to the appropriate data rights or other IP clauses and language. Policy changes and increased staff resources will be required to eliminate or mitigate the effects of this capability gap. IP attorneys would be needed to review the contracts and related acquisition and procurement documentation.

Alternatively, contract and program personnel would require more-extensive training to spot these IP issues so that the issues can be properly flagged and routed to IP attorneys for review. Moreover, these types of IP issues should be addressed early in the solicitation and acquisition process so that contracts and documentation can be drafted correctly from the beginning. Also, a contract and procurement tracking system or database (DHS-wide) would benefit all components and offices in DHS as a tool to capture and build on this information and institutional knowledge as technologies continue to advance.

Invention Secrecy Act
Related Goals and Objectives: 1 (1.1 through 1.4), 2 (2.1 through 2.6), and 3 (3.1 through 3.3)

CWMD is not currently engaged in ISA reviews. However, CWMD's IP attorneys confirmed the need to review patents related to detection devices because it is possible to reverse-engineer the current detection technology. This current vulnerability would expose CWMD, its stakeholders, and U.S. national security to significant risks. Additionally, CWMD works with other entities (e.g., CBP, TSA, the USCG, ICE, the U.S. Department of Energy) both within and outside DHS that develop and deploy detection technology. To be a productive partner, CWMD would likely need to review patents related to detection technology that is within the mission scope of these other agencies.

U.S. Customs and Border Protection

Overview and Mission

CBP is charged with protecting the U.S. border, with a focus on knowing the people, goods, and materials crossing into and out of the country. Created in 2003, CBP combined functions previously performed by what was then the U.S. Customs Service, including immigration inspectors, agricultural inspectors, and border patrol agents (CBP, 2017e). Its mission is "to safeguard America's borders thereby protecting the public from dangerous people and materials while enhancing the Nation's global economic competitiveness by enabling legitimate trade and travel" (CBP, 2019b).

CBP is, first and foremost, a law enforcement agency. In its own words,

> On a typical day, CBP welcomes nearly one million visitors, screens more than 67,000 cargo containers, arrests more than 1,100 individuals, and seizes nearly 6 tons of illicit drugs. Annually, CBP facilitates an average of more than $3 trillion in legitimate trade while enforcing U.S. trade laws. (CBP, 2019b)

CBP's organizational structure consists of four mission-driven jurisdictional divisions and two operations and enterprise service support divisions. The jurisdictional areas are Air and Marine Operations, Field Operations, U.S. Border Patrol, and Trade. Each division is headed by an official at the rank of executive assistant commissioner. In addition, the Laboratories and Scientific Services division supports CBP, providing "forensic and scientific testing in the area of Trade Enforcement, Weapons of Mass Destruction, Intellectual Property Rights, and Narcotics Enforcement" (CBP, 2017a). Figure A.3 provides CBP's organizational chart.

Figure A.3
U.S. Customs and Border Protection Organizational Chart

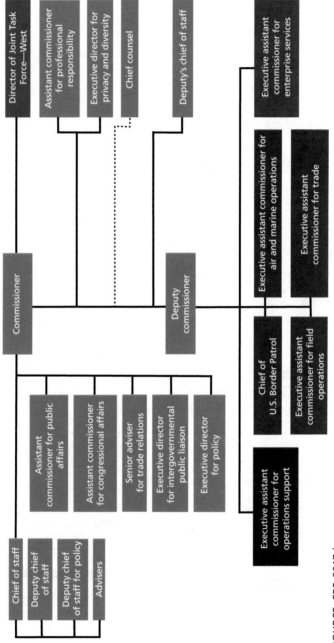

SOURCE: CBP, 2017d.

CBP has four overarching strategic goals, with associated objectives, that define and refine the ways in which it fulfills its mission (CBP, 2015):

- Goal 1: Counter terrorism and transnational crime.
  - Objective 1.1: Understand the threat environment through intelligence and targeting, threat detection, effective enforcement, and border-centric partnerships that can respond to criminal network threats.
  - Objective 1.2: Enhance procedures and partnerships that facilitate interagency and international border enforcement coordination, including data collection, processing, and exploitation.
  - Objective 1.3: Strengthen global supply-chain security.
- Goal 2: Advance comprehensive border security and management.
  - Objective 2.1: Increase situational awareness of the air, land, and maritime borders, including use of the best technological solutions and robust partnerships with local communities and security partners.
  - Objective 2.2: Detect, interdict, and disrupt illegal cross-border activities.
  - Objective 2.3: Strengthen comprehensive trade enforcement, including strengthening capabilities, tools, and techniques for identifying high-risk shipments.
  - Objective 2.4: Strengthen processes to conduct out-bound enforcement and interdiction of travelers and cargo, including partnerships with allied nations.
  - Objective 2.5: Advance a comprehensive predictive targeting strategy to identify threats as early as possible.
- Goal 3: Enhance U.S. economic competitiveness by enabling lawful trade and travel.
  - Objective 3.1: Reduce costs for the U.S. government and the trade and travel communities by streamlining processes in collaboration with public- and private-sector partners—including technological solutions for data input and transmission and associated analysis.

- Objective 3.2: Promote harmonization throughout ports of entry and other U.S. government agencies.
- Objective 3.3: Expand risk segmentation through advanced technology to enable low-risk trade and travel, relying on data and advanced analytics.
• Goal 4: Promote organizational integration, innovation, and agility.
  - Objective 4.1: Mature CBP's strategic resource management framework.
  - Objective 4.2: Optimize CBP's organizational structure to ensure agile and efficient operations.
  - Objective 4.3: Strengthen CBP's culture of unwavering integrity and professional growth.
  - Objective 4.4: Advance CBP mission effectiveness through transformative technologies and innovative business practices.

We found that each of CBP's goals and related objectives has an IP dimension that can aid in facilitating program and mission successes. CBP's reliance on innovative technologies indicates an increasing need for active management of IP considerations. This management should include IP that CBP generates and shares with industry, government, and international partners.

We collected the information in the rest of this section during an interview with CBP officials familiar with IP topics on November 8, 2018.

Current Intellectual Property Portfolio, Staffing, and Needs

CBP's IP needs are necessarily complex. With a history deeply tied to many predecessor organizations, and a future ever-more reliant on technological capabilities for detection, threat prediction, tracking, and border monitoring, CBP already has significant IP dependencies. As criminal networks, smugglers, and terrorists become more technologically sophisticated, CBP will need to scale innovation to meet these new threats. IP management and planning will likely become a more important dimension of activity across CBP because this function offers assets in service to the agency mission.

CBP's IP efforts started in 2018 and thus are still relatively new. As of this writing, predominantly three lawyers, one a former patent attorney, manage the component's IP matters under the Office of Chief Counsel. CBP attorneys do not handle only IP issues, however; the three attorneys work out of the trade and finance office, addressing IP matters on an as-needed basis. The rest of this section describes the types of IP issues on which CBP attorneys presently work.

Patent Litigation
Related Goals and Objectives: 2 (2.2 through 2.5), 3 (3.1 and 3.3), and 4 (3.4)
Although CBP does not have an active program for patent acquisition, it is regularly engaged as a defendant in lawsuits that allege that CBP has infringed the patents of third-party patent holders. This gap indicates the need for increased involvement with IP assets in CBP.

Trademark Enforcement
Related Goals and Objectives: 1 (1.2), 2 (2.3), and 3 (3.1)
Trademark matters are a regular part of CBP's current IP workflow. These matters include applications for new trademarks on program materials and trademark-enforcement actions initiated against third-party entities that misappropriate CBP trademark materials. CBP attorneys have estimated that they will need to respond to about 15 trademark matters each year.

An illustrative example of trademark enforcement demonstrates both the types of issues that have arisen and their connection to program goals. CBP operates CTPAT, a supply-chain safety certification program. Designed to leverage the partnerships between CBP and industry, the program helps provide increased security, implementation of best practices, and close coordination with agency officials and the business community. When an entity joins CTPAT, the entity agrees to work with CBP to protect the supply chain, identify security gaps, and implement specific security measures and best practices. Applicants must comply with a broad range of security topics and present security profiles that list action plans to align security throughout the supply chain. CTPAT members are considered to be of low risk and are therefore less likely to be examined at U.S. ports of entry (CBP, 2019a).

CTPAT certification grants some desirable benefits to industry, including shorter wait times and special relationships with CBP program offices. However, the CTPAT trademark has been misappropriated by several businesses seeking to profit from fraudulent claims of affiliation with the program. In instances in which misappropriation occurs, these actions can lead to the erosion of trust and support for the CTPAT effort by the industry partners that CBP has identified as critical allies for securing the global supply links. Other trademark matters go to the heart of program recognition and effectiveness. Global Entry, the CBP program "that allows expedited clearance for pre-approved, low-risk travelers upon arrival in the United States," also has a trademarked name (CBP, 2017b). However, *NEXUS*, the name of the CPB program that allows expedited passage between the United States and Canada, is not trademarked because of issues arising from the related international treaty between the two countries (CBP, 2017c). Given that both countries "own" the IP from NEXUS, CBP has not been able to secure registration of the mark. The challenges and process roadblocks to improvement within these programs will be contingent on further integration of IP assets.

CBP occasionally finds itself on the other side of trademark-enforcement matters, thus requiring defensive legal support. One instance involved the MMP, a humanitarian initiative that uses locator markers to assist lost and endangered migrants who need emergency assistance.[5] The locator markers used the iconic red cross to broadcast that medical assistance was available. However, per the Geneva Conventions, only the ICRC may use the red cross and red crescent symbols (ICRC, undated). The ICRC issued a cease-and-desist letter to CBP for use of the red cross in the MMP. The CBP IP attorneys handled the matter, continuing to play an educational and informational role in the appropriate use of trademarked materials.

---

[5] For information on the MMP, see CBP, 2018.

Acquisition, Procurement, and Contracts
Related Goals and Objectives: 2 (2.1 through 2.5), 3 (3.1 through 3.3), and 4 (4.1)

Although other DHS components frequently encounter IP issues in procurement activities, CBP's responsibilities do not require similar procurement needs. Instead, CBP is heavily reliant on technology that is purchased off the shelf, as opposed to customized products developed to meet specific needs. As such, commercial licensing efforts represent clearer and more-standardized processes. Moreover, because CBP does not focus heavily on R&D, CBP employees and contractors do not regularly acquire invention disclosures. However, it is not clear whether any inventions should be disclosed but are not; CBP attorneys reported not having been notified of disclosures, not having actively sought to patent CBP inventions, and believing that the number of CBP-generated inventions was likely to be low.

Invention Secrecy Act
Related Goals and Objectives: 1 (1.1 through 1.3) and 2 (2.1 through 2.5)

CBP does not currently engage in ISA reviews. However, CBP counsel indicated that the agency maintains growing interest in reviewing patents that affect its mission set related to national security. In particular, technological capabilities related to sensors, unmanned aircraft systems and counter–unmanned aircraft systems, data encryption, and cargo screening could affect CBP's operational capabilities to combat terrorism and transnational crime. Thus, the ability to conduct ISA review of patents stands as a future need for CBP operations.

Cybersecurity and Infrastructure Security Agency

Overview and Mission
The Cybersecurity and Infrastructure Security Agency Act of 2018 (Pub. L. 115-278) elevated what was then DHS's National Protection and Programs Directorate (NPPD) to a new DHS component, CISA. NPPD was established in 2007 and was responsible for the protection of critical-infrastructure assets, with a specific focus on enhancements

to system resilience (DHS, 2018b). CISA is the successor to this mission and consists of the following divisions (DHS, undated):

- Cybersecurity "works with government and private sector customers to ensure the security and resilience of the Nation's cyber infrastructure." The Cybersecurity Division operates the National Cybersecurity and Communications Integration Center, which provides cyber situational awareness, analysis, incident response, and cyber defense capabilities.
- Emergency Communications "enhances public safety interoperable communications at all levels of government." The Emergency Communications Division works with stakeholders nationwide to promote emergency responders' ability to communicate during disasters, terrorist attacks, and other incidents.
- The Federal Protective Service "protects federal facilities, their occupants, and visitors."
- Infrastructure Security "coordinates security and resilience efforts using trusted partnerships across the private and public sectors." This division performs risk analysis for U.S. critical infrastructure through the National Risk Management Center.[6]

According to NPPD's 2013 National Infrastructure Protection Plan (DHS, 2013), the agency's goals are as follows:

- Goal 1: Assess and analyze threats to, vulnerabilities of, and consequences to critical infrastructure to inform risk management activities.
- Goal 2: Secure critical infrastructure against human, physical, and cyber threats through sustainable efforts to reduce risk while accounting for the costs and benefits of security investments.
- Goal 3: Enhance critical-infrastructure resilience by minimizing the adverse consequences of incidents through advance planning

---

[6] According to CISA, the National Risk Management Center "works to identify and address the most significant risks to our nation's critical infrastructure" (DHS, undated).

and mitigation efforts and employing effective responses to save lives, and ensure the rapid recovery of essential services.

- Goal 4: Share actionable and relevant information across the critical-infrastructure community to build awareness and enable risk-informed decisionmaking.
- Goal 5: Promote learning and adaptation during and after exercises and incidents.

We collected the information presented in the rest of this section during an interview with an NPPD official familiar with IP topics on November 11, 2018.

Current Intellectual Property Portfolio, Staffing, and Needs

Prior to becoming CISA, NPPD's IP-related activities were limited to procurement-related issues (i.e., acquisition and management of technical data and computer software licenses). In November 2017, NPPD hired its first dedicated IP attorney. Since then, NPPD (now CISA) has added elements of trademark enforcement and patent prosecution to its portfolio of IP-related activities.[7]

Patent Prosecution
Related Goals: 1 and 2

Most CISA-sponsored research occurs in national laboratories, and the responsibility to patent and commercialize the resulting inventions falls to those institutions. However, some CISA employees develop internal technical solutions that can result in patentable inventions. For instance, CISA engineers developed Secure Internet Access and File Transfer, software that detects malware in email attachments. CISA's IP attorney is currently working with the engineers to patent this invention.[8] Our research showed that most CISA employees are not aware that their inventions might be patentable or are not interested in

---

[7] CISA's IP attorney further counsels communications and public affairs employees on avoiding copyright- and trademark-infringement issues.

[8] As of the establishment of CISA in November 2016, the attorney was working with the inventor to complete a provisional patent application, which starts the one-year clock for filing a patent application before the USPTO.

filing patent application because they will not directly benefit.[9] If DHS enacts policies to educate employees and encourage patent applications, CISA expects that patent prosecution work will increase.

Trademark Enforcement
Related Goals: 4 and 5

CISA has registered 13 trademarks with the USPTO—five of which are related to SAFECOM, an emergency communications interoperability system managed by the Emergency Communications Division. SAFECOM was initially formed in 2001 in response to the September 11 terrorist attacks to improve public safety communication systems across the United States. However, DHS did not register the trademark until 2018 (USPTO registrations 5595827 and 87913389). In 2017, NPPD discovered that several businesses had been using SAFECOM-related marks in commerce activities for years and had registered those marks under their businesses. For example, QDS Communications registered SafeCom 911 as a mark in 2016 in connection with that company's sale of wireless communications devices (USPTO registration 87042178). As of November 2018, CISA was in the process of contesting these various SAFECOM trademarks. After years of trademark alterations by business, CISA faces a challenging task of working to mitigate the effects of these competing trademarks, including consumer confusion regarding product affiliation.

Until 2017, NPPD did not have a process for identifying logos and marks requiring trademark registration and protection, and CISA still lacks a formal process to register marks. For instance, registration fees still must be obtained on an ad hoc basis. CISA/NPPD had once relied on S&T to search for potential trademark infringement, but that agreement has ended. Currently, CISA does not systematically enforce its trademarks because it lacks a means of identifying potential infringers.

---

[9]   The resulting patent would belong to the United States.

Acquisition, Procurement, and Contracts
Related Goals: 1 Through 3

Like other DHS components, CISA faces challenges in obtaining IP licenses in connection with procurement. CISA frequently procures software in support of its cybersecurity mission and must manage software licenses. The agency's sole IP attorney supports procurement officers in securing the appropriate license by reviewing high-value contracts and by conducting periodic training on IP issues. However, this unique training has recently been deprioritized because of a perceived lack of institutional support and resources.

Invention Secrecy Act
Related Goals: 1 Through 3

CISA does not currently engage in ISA reviews. However, CISA counsel leadership indicated that the agency maintains a strong interest in reviewing patents that affect its mission set related to national security, critical-infrastructure protection, and threat detection. The agency is interested specifically in technology related to malware, encryption, and machine learning, development of which could affect CISA's operational capabilities to protect U.S. critical infrastructure and manage threat and vulnerability monitoring. Thus, the ability to conduct ISA review of patents stands as a future need for CISA.

Federal Emergency Management Agency

Overview and Mission

President Jimmy Carter issued an executive order to create FEMA on July 20, 1979 (Carter, 1979). FEMA remained an independent entity until 2003, when it became part of DHS. FEMA describes itself as the agency that "coordinates the federal government's role in preparing for, preventing, mitigating the effects of, responding to, and recovering from all domestic disasters, whether natural or man-made, including acts of terror" (Emergency Management Institute, 2017). Since 2003, FEMA has undergone significant reorganization and gained new authority after the challenges of Hurricane Katrina. The Post-

Katrina Emergency Management Reform Act of 2006 (Pub. L. 109-295, Title VI) expanded FEMA's overall mission and provided the agency additional capabilities to address the problems revealed by the experience of Katrina (FEMA, 2019a). The agency's mission is "helping people, before, during, and after disasters." From this mission, FEMA envisions "a prepared and resilient Nation" (FEMA, 2018, p. 6).

FEMA's administrator and assistant administrator direct the agency's functions, with the Office of the Administrator serving as the top level of management. The Office of the Administrator directly oversees six offices: the Office of Disability Integration and Coordination, the Office of Equal Rights, the Office of Chief Financial Officer, the Office of External Affairs, the Office of Policy and Program Analysis, and the Office of National Capital Region Coordination. Subordinate divisions of FEMA include Resilience, Mission Support, U.S. Fire Administration, Office of Response and Recovery, and the agency's ten regional offices. FEMA's administrator is additionally supported by the Office of Chief Counsel and the DHS Center for Faith and Opportunity Initiatives. Figure A.4 shows FEMA's organizational chart.

FEMA has three overarching strategic goals, with associated objectives, that define and refine the ways in which it fulfills its mission (FEMA, 2018):

- Goal 1: Build a culture of preparedness.
  - Objective 1.1: Incentivize investments that reduce risk, including predisaster mitigation, and reduce disaster cost at all levels.
  - Objective 1.2: Close the insurance gap.
  - Objective 1.3: Help people prepare for disasters.
  - Objective 1.4: Better learn from past disasters, improve continuously, and innovate.
- Goal 2: Ready the United States for catastrophic disasters.
  - Objective 2.1: Organize a scalable and capable incident workforce.
  - Objective 2.2: Enhance intergovernmental coordination through FEMA integration teams.

Figure A.4
Federal Emergency Management Agency Organizational Chart

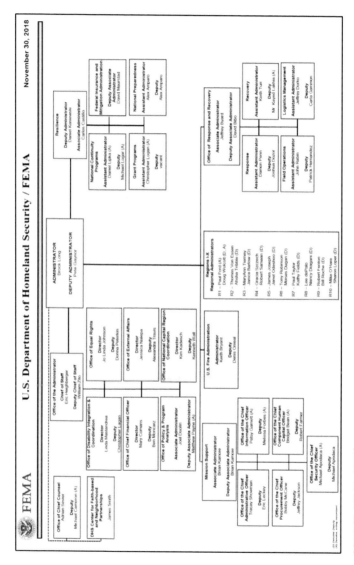

SOURCE: FEMA, 2019b.

- Objective 2.3: Posture FEMA and the whole community to provide lifesaving and life-sustaining commodities, equipment, and personnel from all available sources.
   - Objective 2.4: Improve continuity and resilient communication capabilities.
- Goal 3: Reduce FEMA's complexity.
   - Objective 3.1: Streamline the disaster-survivor and grantee experience.
   - Objective 3.2: Mature the National Disaster Recovery Framework.
   - Objective 3.3: Develop innovative systems and business processes that enable FEMA's employees to rapidly and effectively deliver the agency's mission.
   - Objective 3.4: Strengthen grant management, increase transparency, and improve data analytics.

We collected the information presented in the rest of this section during an interview with FEMA officials familiar with IP topics on December 12, 2018.

Current Intellectual Property Portfolio, Staffing, and Needs

Currently, FEMA has one full-time IP counsel. However, because of the high number of patent suits with which FEMA is involved, this person spends approximately 40 percent of official time managing activities related to litigation issues. IP counsel for FEMA says that IP activities require more than a single full-time equivalent and that sufficient demand exists to support another IP position. In addition to patent litigation, the most-significant demands are found within trademark and copyright issues, data-rights issues, and IP training. IP counsel has noted that, when training is provided, the workload increases dramatically as FEMA staff become more aware of patent, trademark, copyright, and acquisition and procurement issues that require IP legal review or advice.

It is important to note that FEMA maintains a total workforce of approximately 33,000 people (U.S. Government Accountability Office, 2018). This number includes federal employees, as well as additional "surge" and "corps" term-limited employees who assist when disasters occur or other needs arise (U.S. Government Accountability Office, 2018). This large workforce performs a mission set in which IP issues occur with high frequency. Our interviews revealed that the IP office's workload so dramatically increases that the office is "completely swamped." This dynamic indicates a strong latent need for increased IP resources within the agency. Increasing resources to respond to this need might be in the agency's best interest for addressing many of FEMA's challenges.

Copyright
Related Goals and Objectives: 1 (1.4), 2 (2.1 and 2.2), and 3 (3.2, 3.3, and 3.4)

Given that FEMA must employ and train thousands of full-time and temporary employees to staff disaster response operations, staff training and education is a critical and constant demand. The curricula for this training are produced by agency experts and a variety of contractors who provide specific subject-matter knowledge and materials. IP counsel for FEMA says that, when these contractor and vendor agreements are generated, the copyright clauses and conditions are not sufficiently reviewed. As a result, the agency is frequently limited by inappropriate and costly provisions that create roadblocks to critical dissemination when knowledge needs arise.

Additionally, the agency has been challenged with regard to the production of its own education and training materials. Because they lack general understanding on existing copyright and trademark law, employees have produced training documents that include copyrighted and trademarked material without obtaining appropriate permissions. One example included the inappropriate use of Marvel Comics IP in a training tool that was widely distributed. These violations increase the risk of costly liability and litigation conflicts for the agency. We believe that the inability to sufficiently review vendor contracts and the pattern of oversights in training and education materials are directly related to the lack of agency IP staff.

Trademark Registration and Enforcement
Related Goals and Objectives: 1 (1.1 through 1.4) and 2 (2.3 and 2.4)

FEMA currently possesses 14 trademarks. Additionally, although the name *FEMA* is not trademarked, the agency has made a concerted effort to use common law enforcement mechanisms to protect the use of the name. Trademarks and trademark enforcement are areas of top concern for agency leadership. FEMA has recognized that infringement of the agency's marks frequently takes place in disaster areas when populations are in their greatest need. Anecdotally, it has been reported that unscrupulous individuals and groups seek to use FEMA-related marks to present their products as coming from or being certified by FEMA. For example, fraudulent vendors have misappropriated FEMA's National Flood Insurance Program materials to sell insurance to consumers, even when the insurance is not necessarily consistent with national standards. Given the lack of IP support, FEMA officials are not in a position to actively police these infractions. As a result, FEMA largely relies on the public to report on the many instances of outright fraud that have been committed.

FEMA actively seeks to prevent these abuses by issuing cease-and-desist letters and policing websites that misappropriate FEMA marks and the FEMA name. Currently, the agency has been able to remove between five and ten websites per year by actively searching for the misuse and responding to reports of fraud. The cost of this website monitoring has been approximately $6,000 per year. However, IP counsel reports that these efforts are currently understaffed and underfunded. Counsel believes that, with more-active search measures, the number of enforcement actions could significantly increase.

Patent Litigation
Related Goals and Objectives: 1 (1.1), 2 (2.3 and 2.4), and 3 (3.3 and 3.4)

As noted above, FEMA IP counsel spends approximately 40 percent of official time on managing patent-related litigation conflicts for the agency. The majority of this time is spent assisting DOJ attorneys who are responsible for defending FEMA in federal court. Our research found that such duties as court filings, document review, depositions, and evidence collection and management are the more time-consuming tasks that are involved. Approximately one or two patent-infringement suits are brought against FEMA per year. Many of these suits involve complex software and communication systems that FEMA uses and deploys in disaster and emergency situations.

IP counsel anticipates that the number of lawsuits could rise. FEMA's mission scope and workforce size have grown consistently for several years.[10] As the agency becomes more active in the public sphere, patent holders will have more opportunity to suspect that FEMA has engaged in activities that infringe on their patents. HSOAC is not in a position to evaluate this supposition. However, given the number of work hours that IP counsel spends on one or two cases per year, even a small increase in litigation conflict could severely affect the agency's ability to meet all of its other IP-related needs.

Acquisition, Procurement, and Contracts

Related Goals and Objectives: 1 (1.3 and 1.4), 2 (2.1 through 2.4), and 3 (3.1 through 3.4)

FEMA currently maintains a $500,000 threshold for the requirement of legal review for acquisition and procurement contracts. Above this threshold, the contracts are reviewed by FEMA's Office of Chief Counsel but are not necessarily examined by IP counsel. IP counsel reports that this is a significant area of risk for the agency. FEMA invests in a large amount of software and communication systems for employees and first responders. These contracts frequently lack the appropriate data-rights, maintenance, and development conditions and clauses that FEMA needs in order to maintain operational capability at the lowest possible costs. There is a substantive need to perform an IP review of these contracts, as well as for bids below the $500,000 threshold.

---

[10] As referenced above, FEMA's workforce was approximately 33,000 in January 2018. That number stood at 7,558 in 2005. See U.S. Government Accountability Office, 2015.

Invention Secrecy Act
Related Goals and Objectives: 1 (1.3), 3 (3.3), 4 (4.1 and 4.2), and 5 (5.1 and 5.2)

FEMA does not currently engage in ISA reviews. However, FEMA IP counsel has indicated that the agency is interested in reviewing patents that affect its mission set with regard to the integrity of communications during national emergencies and disasters. In particular, technology related to sustaining continuity of operations, broadcast communications, cell phones, and broadband platforms could affect FEMA's operational capabilities to protect vulnerable populations and operational personnel and equipment when deploying to and assisting in disaster areas. Thus, the ability to conduct ISA review of patents stands as a future need for FEMA.

Federal Law Enforcement Training Center

Overview and Mission

FLETC began in 1970 as a bureau under the U.S. Department of the Treasury. The center was created to address inconsistencies found in the training practices of federal law enforcement officers. Because the quality of federal law enforcement is viewed as critical to U.S. security, the center was transferred from the Treasury Department to DHS in 2003 (FLETC, undated). FLETC serves as the largest law enforcement training program in the country, working with partner agencies and organizations to supply training in law enforcement topics for local, state, tribal, and federal entities. FLETC's mission is to "train those who protect the homeland" (FLETC, 2016, p. 4). The training of law enforcement officers extends well beyond the federal government to include those at the state, local, tribal, and international levels. Because FLETC trains a variety of officers for a diverse set of operational tasks, its mission engages with all facets of DHS objectives (FLETC, 2016, pp. 6–7, 9).

FLETC is managed by a director, deputy director, chief of staff, and chief counsel. FLETC has four operational divisions: Centralized Training Management, Glynco Training, Regional and International

Training, and Training Research and Innovation (FLETC, 2016, p. 10).[11] The organizational chart in Figure A.5 shows the supporting structure for these divisions.

Three of FLETC's goals and their supporting objectives aid the center in fulfilling its mission (FLETC, 2016, pp. 48–51):

- Goal 1: Lead a global training effort to meet the emerging and dynamic goals of law enforcement.
    - Objective 1.1: Advance the principles of consolidated and collaborative training to yield quantitative and qualitative results.
    - Objective 1.2: Infuse contemporary and emerging concepts into FLETC training in partnership with federal, state, local, tribal, and international law enforcement.
    - Objective 1.3: Institutionalize FLETC's virtual training environment to enhance, extend, and complement FLETC's training capabilities.

Figure A.5
Federal Law Enforcement Training Centers Organizational Chart

SOURCE: FLETC, 2016, p. 10.

---

[11] FLETC is headquartered in Glynco, Georgia.

- – Objective 1.4: Integrate research-based curricula and technology to ensure that training meets contemporary and future law enforcement mission needs.
- – Objective 1.5: Advance the U.S. government's homeland security goals through training and capacity-building with federal, state, local, tribal, international, and private-sector security agencies.
- Goal 2: Cultivate a diverse community that is continuously learning and engaged in the FLETC mission.
  - – Objective 2.1: Pursue opportunities for professional education, training, and development to maximize individual potential in support of the FLETC mission.
  - – Objective 2.2: Engage with partners to better anticipate and meet their needs.
  - – Objective 2.3: Understand and enhance the quality of employee engagement.
  - – Objective 2.4: Pursue recruitment and retention strategies to ensure that FLETC has the right talent to accomplish its mission.
- Goal 3: Strengthen FLETC's business processes and assets to effectively accomplish all related homeland security goals.
  - – Objective 3.1: Pursue excellence in business practices.
  - – Objective 3.2: Utilize data analytics to effectively and efficiently meet the FLETC mission.
  - – Objective 3.3: Ensure that FLETC has sufficient and appropriate technical, human capital, and physical capabilities to meet future training and homeland security requirements.
  - – Objective 3.4: Share expertise in support of DHS lines of business.

We compiled the information presented in the rest of this section during an interview with a FLETC attorney familiar with IP topics on November 19, 2018.

Current Intellectual Property Portfolio, Staffing, and Needs

FLETC's IP portfolio is currently limited in scope, with the delegated IP attorney working on a variety of IP-related matters as they arise. FLETC currently has six lawyers working as general counsel for the agency, and one attorney has been charged with handling IP matters. The attorney handles IP issues on an as-needed basis, dedicating approximately 5 percent of the position's time to these efforts. When more-complex IP matters arise, the FLETC attorney works directly with OGC/IP to address them on a prorated basis.

Patent Litigation and Prosecution
Related Goals: Supporting Departmentwide Missions

According to FLETC's IP attorney, the center has been involved in cases of patent infringement in the past. However, OGC manages these cases, and DOJ represents the center in court. During the cases, FLETC lawyers support DOJ by delivering contracting documents for review, gathering any needed information, and providing relevant POCs. In the past ten years, the FLETC IP attorney has supported approximately four or five of these types of cases. Most of the cases have been handled at the department level and require FLETC participation, rather than being cases targeted specifically at the center.

Trademark Management
Related Goals: 1 Through 3

FLETC's connection to law enforcement and its role as a trainer for enforcement officers at all levels of government make its name and symbols potential targets for misuse and misappropriation. Although the center did not believe that it had faced any formal trademark violations, the IP attorney noted that the center has found external parties highlighting or using their connection to FLETC on public materials and websites. To combat these types of actions, FLETC includes a clause in its contracts to prevent partners from capitalizing on the FLETC name and reputation. The FLETC attorney works with OGC/IP to handle any instances of unauthorized use of the FLETC name, symbol, or other related imagery.

Procurement

Goals: 1 Through 3

FLETC's responsibilities do not require large procurement contracts, thus limiting the need for procurement-related IP management. Furthermore, many of the center's training materials are developed in house, consequently avoiding the potential for licensing challenges with external contractors. The FLETC attorney provided one example of difficulty, however, in working with a third-party company due to changes made to commercial, off-the-shelf software. FLETC believed that the alterations made to the software fell within the parameters of the license agreement, while the issuing company contended otherwise. The attorney we interviewed also acknowledged that limits on software licenses had caused difficulties at times with the center's financial management system. Although procurement issues have not been a large point of contention for FLETC yet, the IP attorney noted concern about the potential for this risk to increase over time and the consequential need for additional IP support to handle this increased risk.

Invention Secrecy Act

FLETC does not currently engage in ISA reviews.

U.S. Immigration and Customs Enforcement

Overview and Mission

ICE formed in 2003 through the Homeland Security Act of 2002 (Pub. L. 107-296). ICE combined the investigative and interior enforcement elements from two prior federal agencies: the U.S. Customs Service and INS (ICE, 2018d). ICE includes more than 20,000 law enforcement officers and support personnel in more than 400 offices across the United States. The agency operates under the following mission statement: "to protect America from the cross-border crime and illegal immigration that threaten national security and public safety" (ICE, 2018c). ICE identifies three key areas that support its mission:

immigration enforcement, investigating illegal movement of people and goods, and preventing terrorism (ICE, 2018c).

To carry out this mission and address the three key areas, ICE is organized into three operational directorates: HSI, Enforcement and Removal Operations (ERO), and Office of the Principal Legal Advisor (OPLA). HSI serves as the principal investigative component of DHS, operating in more than 45 countries. HSI agents manage cross-border investigations to address potential threats to U.S. national security. ERO works to enforce and support U.S. immigration law within and outside of U.S. territory. It focuses on public safety threats and the immigration enforcement process, seeking to thwart those who pose a threat to national security and public safety. OPLA provides the attorneys and legal support for all immigration removal screenings. It employs more than 1,100 lawyers, making up the largest legal program in DHS. In addition to representing ICE during proceedings, OPLA supplies counsel and legal support for all offices within ICE (ICE, 2018d).

ICE also operates the National Intellectual Property Rights Coordination Center (National Intellectual Property Rights Coordination Center, undated a). The center is a statutorily required effort, coordinated across "19 key federal agencies, Interpol [the International Criminal Police Organization], Europol [the European Union Agency for Law Enforcement Cooperation], and the governments of Canada and Mexico," with the mission "to ensure national security by protecting the public's health and safety, the U.S. economy, and our war fighters, and to stop predatory and unfair trade practices that threaten the global economy" (National Intellectual Property Rights Coordination Center, undated b). The target of the center's activities is the theft of IP through fake, fraudulent, and counterfeit goods. Ironically, as discussed in more detail below, ICE itself does not have an IP specialist on staff in its chief counsel division.

ICE does not have a strategic plan publicly available, so we could not include information on its goals, objectives, and organizational structure here. Figure A.6 presents its organizational chart.

Figure A.6
U.S. Immigration and Customs Enforcement Organizational Chart

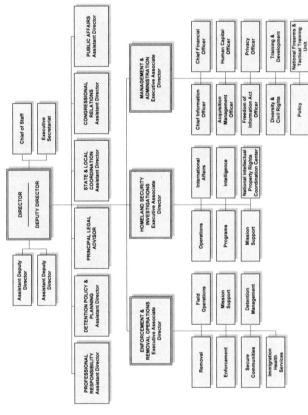

SOURCE: DHS, 2011.

We collected the information presented in the rest of this section during an interview with ICE officials familiar with IP topics on November 8, 2018.

Current Intellectual Property Portfolio, Staffing, and Needs

Currently, OPLA has one assigned attorney responsible for IP matters for the agency. The person in this position reported that most of the time spent on IP duties related to procurement, acquisition, and contract review. As a large law enforcement agency, ICE spends a significant amount of its budget, approximately $2.4 billion, on thousands of types of contracts (DHS, 2018a). Additionally, ICE operations involve nearly all aspects of IP functions, including patents, trademarks, copyrights, and invention disclosure. ICE IP counsel further indicated that ICE's national security mission might also support ISA efforts. Patent-infringement litigation is another area that requires significant IP counsel resources. Additionally, when not consumed with other IP duties, ICE IP counsel attempts to provide ICE personnel with as much IP training as possible. In sum, sufficient need appears to exist to support the addition of at least one additional IP counsel.

Copyright

Related Goals and Objectives: Not Applicable (strategic plan is not publicly available)

ICE is a law enforcement organization of approximately 20,000 law enforcement agents, staff, and personnel. ICE is required to conduct a significant amount of training, particularly for its law enforcement agents. As such, the use of contractor- and vendor-provided materials in training and operations is highly standardized. However, ICE is frequently limited in its use of these materials by IP-related clauses and conditions in vendor contracts. In some cases, the copyright restrictions are unnecessarily limited, which hampers ICE's ability to effectively train and educate its personnel. We believe that a more thorough review and negotiation of these clauses and conditions could significantly improve ICE's training and knowledge-management programs.

Trademark Registration and Enforcement

Related Goals and Objectives: Not Applicable (strategic plan is not publicly available)

As law enforcement efforts that involve partnerships with other public and private entities grow in size and number, the opportunity for ICE to trademark materials related to these efforts are likely to grow as well. ICE currently holds one trademark with respect to the National Intellectual Property Coordination Center, which enforces U.S. criminal IP laws. However, IP counsel noted that both DHS and ICE seals are frequently misused by DHS and ICE contractors and by bad actors seeking either to pose as law enforcement agents or to operate in a manner that implies ICE approval or certification. IP counsel believes that more could be done to combat the misappropriation and misuse of these marks and seals. In this way, trademarks are a tool for ICE to expand its footprint in the community, which, in turn, allows it to better engage with the public for the purposes of combating crimes related to its broad jurisdiction. Additional resources would be required to identify, file, and then protect these trademarks as well.

Patent Litigation

Related Goals and Objectives: Not Applicable (strategic plan is not publicly available

As noted above, one area of IP that consumes ICE IP counsel's time is patent litigation. Currently, ICE is involved in six patent-infringement cases. Numerous other infringement actions have been threatened, but litigation has been avoided through negotiated settlements. In many cases, ICE has not been the primary respondent but has become part of the lawsuit after filing because it uniformly applies the same law enforcement techniques or materials that the initial subjects of the suits (law enforcement agencies) use. This dynamic makes the number and frequency of these actions extremely difficult to predict.

Moreover, ICE currently holds two patents having to do with firearm training and two additional patents pending having to do with X-ray belt photography and anticounterfeiting measures. It is conceivable that ICE will need to affirmatively protect these patents from infringement. Equally important is that ICE operates the HSI Forensic

Laboratory. Personnel at the lab have recently become aware that they have the option to patent their work. As a result, ICE recently filed seven new patents to claim its asset rights. ICE IP counsel estimates that the HSI lab (by itself) could file three to five patent applications per year based on the work product of laboratory experts. This increase in the number of patent filings could justify the addition of another IP attorney at ICE.

Acquisition, Procurement, and Contracts
Related Goals and Objectives: Not Applicable (strategic plan is not publicly available)
ICE IP counsel noted that the lack of review of ICE acquisition and procurement contracts for IP purposes was a "grave detriment" to the agency. Agency operations have frequently been impeded by contractor and vendor agreements that prevent ICE from exercising appropriate IP rights. These conflicts range from challenges with data rights to continued development of the underlying technology or product. The lack of review of these contracts, and the resulting restrictions placed on ICE, not only have been costly but have impeded ICE's ability to operate optimally. For example, a current single-source contract has caused a dispute with respect to a particular set of data rights. In this case, the dispute has inhibited ICE's ability to use data and information collected on its own law enforcement operations to combat gangs and transnational criminal organizations. IP counsel believes that a specific review of all major ICE contracts for IP-related language, clauses, and conditions is required to ensure that ICE can contract effectively and in a manner that promotes operational capability.

Invention Secrecy Act
Related Goals and Objectives: Not Applicable (strategic plan is not publicly available)
ICE does not currently engage in ISA reviews. However, ICE IP counsel has indicated that the agency maintains interests in reviewing patents that affect its mission functions related to its national security and law enforcement mission sets. In particular, ICE will seek to invest in technology that relates to cybercrime (e.g., "dark web" activities), crypto-currencies (for use in illicit activities), money laundering, cell

phone technology and encryption, and document security features. Certain patents in these areas could affect ICE's operational capabilities to protect the United States and combat terrorism and transnational crime. Thus, the ability to conduct ISA review of patents in these areas stands as a future need for ICE.

Transportation Security Administration

Overview and Mission

Established in 2001 as a response to the September 11, 2001, terrorist attacks, TSA is tasked with "protecting the nation's transportation systems to ensure freedom of movement for people and commerce" (TSA, 2018a, p. 2). Although it was initially part of the U.S. Department of Transportation, TSA became part of the then–newly created DHS in 2002.

TSA's primary task is screening air passengers and baggage. In its total workforce of approximately 60,000, TSA employs more than 50,000 transportation security officers who screen more than 2 million air travelers each day. TSA further inspects hundreds of U.S. and international airports and collaborates with surface transportation stakeholders to improve security for mass transit, railways, highways, and pipelines. In its *2018 Biennial National Strategy for Transportation Security*, TSA announced three overarching strategic goals, each with associated priorities (TSA, 2018b, pp. 12–15):

- Goal 1: Manage risks to transportation systems from terrorist attacks, and enhance system reliance.
    - Priority 1.1: Develop physical security measures to close gaps identified by risk assessments.
    - Priority 1.2: Prevent introduction of WMD and other lethal weapons into transportation systems.
    - Priority 1.3: Encourage assessment of threats to cyber systems and appropriate mitigation investments.

- Priority 1.4: Emphasize screening and vetting measures, such as biometric facial recognition, personnel security assessments, and credentialing programs.
- Priority 1.5: Recognize that successful measures depend on well-trained and informed personnel.

• Goal 2: Enhance effective domain awareness of transportation systems and threats.
- Priority 2.1: Assess current threats and other indicators to address and mitigate risks.
- Priority 2.2: Analyze and distribute information collected through assessments.
- Priority 2.3: Coordinate operations through multiple preparedness mission areas.
- Priority 2.4: Hone proper security awareness and procedures.

• Goal 3: Safeguard privacy, civil liberties, and civil rights; and the freedom of movement of people and commerce.
- Priority 3.1: Use technology, data, and analytic methods to make risk-based decisions on the necessary level of screening.
- Priority 3.2: Ensure that screening procedures accommodate personal circumstances of travelers while preserving security.
- Priority 3.3: Apply strict security protocols to protect sensitive information.

All three of TSA's strategic goals emphasize increased reliance on technological solutions. TSA will need to properly manage associated IP in order to effectively develop and deploy innovative processes.

We collected the information presented in the rest of this section during an interview with TSA officials familiar with IP topics on November 13, 2018.

Current Intellectual Property Portfolio, Staffing, and Needs

Much of TSA's IP-related work supports procurement activities (i.e., obtaining and managing appropriate IP and licenses from contractors). TSA further maintains some trademarks with the USPTO and was the defendant in a recent multiyear patent-infringement lawsuit (see SecurityPoint discussion next). TSA's IP matters fall under the responsibility of a single IP attorney from S&T who has formally been on detail to TSA since 2012. The detailed attorney also directly supports TSA procurement contracts with producers of training material, which involves certain copyright issues. TSA's attorney routinely reviews other procurement contracts for IP issues.

Patent Litigation
Related Goals and Priorities: 1 (1.1 through 1.3) and 3 (3.1 and 3.3)
In 2011, SecurityPoint filed a lawsuit against TSA in the U.S. Court of Federal Claims for infringement of a patent that covers a method for recycling security trays at airport checkpoints. TSA stipulated to infringement but argued that the underlying patent was invalid. The Court of Federal Claims, however, upheld the patent's validity, and TSA faced significant compensation payouts (*SecurityPoint*, 2016, p. 28).[12] This was the first major patent-infringement lawsuit that TSA faced. DOJ litigated the lawsuit on TSA's behalf, and TSA added the detailed IP attorney to coordinate with DOJ.

Trademark Management
Related Goals and Priorities: 2 (2.2 through 2.4) and 3 (3.3)
TSA collaborates with S&T to identify potential trademark infringement. TSA components have developed public-facing programs that aim to improve security screening. For instance, TSA Pre✓ enables an air traveler who voluntarily undergoes a security threat assessment to be eligible for expedited screening at airports. And TSA issues credentials (e.g., the Transportation Worker Identification Credential, or TWIC) to workers who are required to have access to sensitive areas within the transportation infrastructure. TSA has found it necessary to register program names and logos with the USPTO in order to prevent consumer confusion.

---

[12] TSA appealed, and the Federal Circuit held that the appeal was premature because the Court of Federal Claims had not resolved all of TSA's liabilities (*SecurityPoint Holdings, Inc. v. United States*, No. 17-1421 (Fed. Cir. appeal denied March 9, 2017).

Procurement

Related Goals and Priorities: 1 (1.1 through 1.4) and 3 (3.1 and 3.3)

When TSA was first established, it procured substantial amounts of screening equipment from contractors. It decided not to purchase technical data rights associated with that equipment. As a result of those early decisions, TSA has been required to return to the original equipment manufacturers for maintenance, repair, and upgrade needs. As the original manufacturers, these providers are in monopolist positions and charge prices well above market value for their services.

TSA's sole IP attorney is responsible for reviewing procurement contracts to ensure that they contain appropriate data-rights provisions. The attorney has found that TSA contracting officers do not always understand data-rights provisions. For example, they might include several data-rights clauses that contradict each other or fail to specify how technical data to which TSA has rights should be delivered. The addition of an IP attorney has enabled TSA to catch and remedy some of these errors. However, that attorney reviews only a subset of procurement contracts, typically those in excess of $500,000 in value. TSA's attorney does not routinely scrutinize contractors' restrictive assertions over technical data—for instance, determining the government rights with respect to technology that is derivative of government-funded research.

Invention Secrecy Act

Related Goals and Priorities: 1 (1.2 and 1.4), 2 (2.2), and 3 (3.3)

TSA does not currently engage in ISA reviews. However, TSA counsel leadership indicated that TSA has interests in reviewing patents that affect its mission areas related to national security, securing transportation systems, and threat and vulnerability detection. In particular, TSA will seek to review technology that relates to scanning, data management (specifically, classified data), and data-encryption solutions that could affect TSA's operational capabilities. Thus, the ability to conduct ISA review of patents stands as a future need for TSA.

References

Abercrombie & Fitch Co. v. Hunting World, Inc., 537 F.2d 4 (2d Cir. 1976).

Apple Inc. v. Samsung Elecs. Co., 786 F.3d 983 (Fed. Cir. 2015).

Basel Committee on Banking Supervision, *Customer Due Diligence for Banks*, Bank for International Settlements, October 2001. As of April 27, 2019: https://www.bis.org/publ/bcbs85.pdf

Bilski v. Kappos, 561 U.S. 593 (2010). As of April 27, 2019: https://scholar.google.com/scholar_case?case=18086536145760645965&hl=en&as_sdt=6&as_vis=1&oi=scholar

Bush, George W., "Executive Order 13286 of February 28, 2003: Amendment of Executive Orders, and Other Actions, in Connection with the Transfer of Certain Functions to the Secretary of Homeland Security," *Federal Register*, Vol. 68, No. 43, March 5, 2003, pp. 10617–10633. As of May 16, 2019: https://www.govinfo.gov/app/details/FR-2003-03-05/03-5343

Carter, Jimmy, "Executive Order 12148 of July 20, 1979: Federal Emergency Management," *Federal Register*, Vol. 44, No. 143, July 24, 1979, pp. 43239–43246. As of May 5, 2019: https://www.govinfo.gov/app/details/FR-1979-07-24

CBP—*See* U.S. Customs and Border Protection.

CCC Info Servs. v. MacLean Hunter Mkt. Reports, Inc., 44 F.3d 61 (2d Cir. 1994).

Chertoff, Michael, Secretary, U.S. Department of Homeland Security, "Delegation to the Under Secretary for Science and Technology to Facilitate Technology Transfer," Delegation 10002, October 24, 2005.

Christian Louboutin S.A. v. Yves Saint Laurent Am. Holding, Inc., 696 F.3d 206 (2d Cir. 2012).

Christianson v. Colt Industries Operating Corp., 870 F.2d 1292 (7th Cir. 1989), *cert. denied*, 493 U.S. 822 (1989).

CISA—*See* Cybersecurity and Infrastructure Security Agency.

Code of Federal Regulations, Title 37, Patents, Trademarks, and Copyrights; Chapter I, United States Patent and Trademark Office, Department of Commerce; Subchapter A, General; Part 5, Secrecy of Certain Inventions and Licenses to Export and File Applications in Foreign Countries; Section 5.3, Prosecution of Application Under Secrecy Orders; Withholding Patent, July 1, 2018. As of April 27, 2019:
https://www.govinfo.gov/app/details/CFR-2018-title37-vol1/
CFR-2018-title37-vol1-sec5-3

Code of Federal Regulations, Title 37, Patents, Trademarks, and Copyrights; Chapter IV, National Institute of Standards and Technology, Department of Commerce; Part 401, Rights to Inventions Made by Nonprofit Organizations and Small Business Firms Under Government Grants, Contracts, and Cooperative Agreements. As of May 17, 2019:
https://www.govinfo.gov/app/details/CFR-2018-title37-vol1/
CFR-2018-title37-vol1-part401

Code of Federal Regulations, Title 48, Federal Acquisition Regulations System; Chapter 7, Agency for International Development; Subchapter H, Clauses and Forms; Part 752, Solicitation Provisions and Contract Clauses; Subpart 752.2, Texts of Provisions and Clauses; Section 752.227-14, Rights in Data—General. As of May 11, 2019:
https://www.govinfo.gov/app/details/CFR-2018-title48-vol5/
CFR-2018-title48-vol5-sec752-227-14

Corrigan, Jack, "DHS Awards $1.5M for Algorithms to Accelerate Airport Security," *Nextgov*, July 11, 2018. As of February 12, 2019:
https://www.nextgov.com/emerging-tech/2018/07/
dhs-awards-15m-algorithms-accelerate-airport-security/149608/

Cybersecurity and Infrastructure Security Agency, "Mitigate DNS Infrastructure Tampering," Emergency Directive 19-01, January 22, 2019. As of April 27, 2019:
https://cyber.dhs.gov/ed/19-01/

DHS—*See* U.S. Department of Homeland Security.

Diamond v. Chakrabarty, 447 U.S. 303 (1980).

Diamond v. Diehr, 450 U.S. 175 (1981).

Dilawar, Arvind, "The U.S. Government's Secret Inventions," *Slate*, May 9, 2018. As of February 13, 2019:
https://slate.com/technology/2018/05/
the-thousands-of-secret-patents-that-the-u-s-government-refuses-to-make-public.
html

Director, Office of Public–Private Partnerships, Office of the Deputy Under Secretary of Homeland Security for Science and Technology, U.S. Department of Homeland Security, "Intellectual Property, Technology Transfer and Commercialization Governance, Implementation and Metrics Plan," memorandum, October 19, 2016 (approved November 2, 2016).

eBay Inc. v. MercExchange, L.L.C., 547 U.S. 388 (2006).

Emergency Management Institute, "Emergency Management Institute (EMI) Overview," last modified February 24, 2017. As of May 5, 2019:
https://training.fema.gov/history.aspx

ERBE Elektromedizin GmbH v. Canady Tech. LLC, 629 F.3d 1278 (Fed. Cir. 2010).

FAR 52.227-14—*See* 48 C.F.R. 752.227-14.

Federal Emergency Management Agency, *2018–2022 Strategic Plan: Federal Emergency Management Agency*, Washington, D.C.: U.S. Department of Homeland Security, March 15, 2018. As of April 27, 2019:
https://www.fema.gov/strategic-plan

Federal Emergency Management Agency, "About the Agency," Washington, D.C., last updated January 30, 2019a. As of February 14, 2019:
http://www.fema.gov/about-agency

Federal Emergency Management Agency, "FEMA Leadership Organizational Structure," last updated April 30, 2019b. As of May 5, 2019:
https://www.fema.gov/media-library/assets/documents/28183

Federal Law Enforcement Training Centers, "FLETC History," Washington, D.C., undated. As of February 14, 2019:
https://www.fletc.gov/fletc-history#

Federal Law Enforcement Training Centers, *Strategic Plan: Fiscal Years 2016–2018*, Washington, D.C., c. 2016. As of April 29, 2019:
https://www.fletc.gov/sites/default/files/
FLETC%20Strategic%20Plan%20FY%202016-2018%20FINAL%20508.pdf

Feist Publ'ns, Inc. v. Rural Tel. Serv. Co., 499 U.S. 340 (1991).

FEMA—*See* Federal Emergency Management Agency.

FLETC—*See* Federal Law Enforcement Training Centers.

Historian's Office, U.S. Coast Guard, "Missions," Washington, D.C., undated a.

Historian's Office, U.S. Coast Guard, "U.S. Coast Guard History Program," Washington, D.C., undated b. As of February 13, 2019:
https://www.history.uscg.mil/About/

ICE—*See* U.S. Immigration and Customs Enforcement.

ICRC—*See* International Committee of the Red Cross.

International Committee of the Red Cross, "Copyright and Terms of Use," undated. As of February 14, 2019:
https://www.icrc.org/en/copyright-and-terms-use

Johnson, Bridget, "Deep Commitment at USCIS Day to 'Huge Shift' of Paperless Filing by 2020," *Homeland Security Today*, October 15, 2018. As of February 13, 2019:
https://www.hstoday.us/federal-pages/dhs/uscis-dhs-federal-pages/
deep-commitment-at-uscis-day-to-huge-shift-of-paperless-filing-by-2020/

Johnson, Jeh, Secretary, U.S. Department of Homeland Security, "Delegation to the Under Secretary for Science and Technology," Delegation 10001, Revision 01, April 28, 2014.

Katich, Alexandra H., "Innovation Worth Sharing: Seeking Balance Between Innovation Policy and National Security," *Cardozo Journal of International and Comparative Law*, Vol. 23, No. 2, Winter 2015, pp. 413–446.

KSR Int'l Co. v. Teleflex Inc., 550 U.S. 398 (2007).

Lee, Sabing H., "Protecting the Private Inventor Under the Peacetime Provisions of the Invention Secrecy Act," *Berkeley Technology Law Journal*, Vol. 12, No. 2, 1997, pp. 345–411.

MAI Sys. Corp. v. Peak Computer, Inc., 991 F.2d 511 (9th Cir. 1993).

Maune, James, "Patent Secrecy Orders: Fairness Issues in Application of Invention of Secrecy Act," *Texas Intellectual Property Law Journal*, Vol. 20, No. 3, Summer 2012, pp. 471–491.

Merkle, Dawn Lee, "Is the Golden Goose on the Chopping Block?" Martindale, November 28, 2017. As of February 12, 2019:
https://www.martindale.com/legal-news/article_willcox-savage-pc_2504289.htm

Mitchell, Margaret, *Gone with the Wind*, New York: Macmillan Company, 1936.

Morrissey v. P&G, 379 F.2d 675 (1st Cir. 1967).

National Intellectual Property Rights Coordination Center, homepage, undated a. As of May 5, 2019:
https://www.iprcenter.gov/

National Intellectual Property Rights Coordination Center, "About Us," undated b. As of May 5, 2019:
https://www.iprcenter.gov/about

Nazer, Daniel, "Stupid Patent of the Month: Carrying Trays on a Cart," Electronic Frontier Foundation, December 22, 2016. As of February 12, 2019:
https://www.eff.org/deeplinks/2016/12/stupid-patent-month-carrying-trays-cart

Nielsen, Kirstjen M., Secretary, U.S. Department of Homeland Security, "Delegation to the Assistant Secretary of the Countering of Weapons of Mass Destruction Office," Delegation 2500, May 21, 2018.

Office of Inspector General, U.S. Department of Homeland Security, *USCIS Automation of Immigration Benefits Processing Remains Ineffective*, Washington, D.C., OIG-16-48, March 9, 2016. As of April 27, 2019:
https://www.oig.dhs.gov/reports/2016-03/
uscis-automation-immigration-benefits-processing-remains-ineffective/oig-16-48

Office of the Deputy Under Secretary for Management, U.S. Department of Homeland Security, Department of Homeland Security Directive 112-01, revision 00, April 10, 2008. As of May 16, 2019:
https://www.dhs.gov/sites/default/files/publications/
mgmt_directive_112_01_directives_system.pdf

Office of the General Counsel, U.S. Department of Homeland Security, "Intellectual Property," Department of Homeland Security Directive 012-01, Revision 00, April 1, 2010.

OGC—*See* Office of the General Council.

Oracle Am., Inc. v. Google Inc., 750 F.3d 1339 (Fed. Cir. 2014), *cert. denied*, 135 S. Ct. 2887 (2015).

Publ'ns. Int'l, Ltd. v. Meredith Corp., 88 F.3d 473 (7th Cir. 1996).

Public Law 65-80, an act to prevent the publication of inventions by the grant of patents that might be detrimental to the public safety or convey useful information to the enemy, stimulate invention, and provide adequate protection to owners of patents, and for other purposes, October 6, 1917.

Public Law 71-245, Townsend–Parnell Plant Patent Act of 1930, May 23, 1930.

Public Law 76-700, an act to amend the act relating to preventing the publication of inventions in the national interest and for other purposes, July 1, 1940.

Public Law 79-489, an act to provide for the registration and protection of trademarks used in commerce, to carry out the provisions of certain international conventions, for other purposes, July 5, 1946.

Public Law 82-256, Invention Secrecy Act of 1951, February 1, 1952. As of April 30, 2019:
https://www.govinfo.gov/app/details/STATUTE-66/STATUTE-66-Pg3

Public Law 83-703, Atomic Energy Act of 1954, August 30, 1954. As of May 1, 2019:
https://www.govinfo.gov/app/details/STATUTE-68/STATUTE-68-Pg919

Public Law 91-577, Plant Variety Protection Act of 1970, December 24, 1970.

Public Law 94-553, an act for the general revision of the Copyright Law, Title 17 of the U.S. Code, and for other purposes, October 19, 1976.

Public Law 96-517, an act to amend the patent and trademark laws, December 12, 1980. As of May 17, 2019:
http://uscode.house.gov/statutes/pl/96/517.pdf

Public Law 99-502, Federal Technology Transfer Act of 1986, October 20, 1986. As of May 2, 2019: https://www.govinfo.gov/content/pkg/STATUTE-100/pdf/ STATUTE-100-Pg1785.pdf

Public Law 100-568, Berne Convention Implementation Act of 1988, October 31, 1988. As of April 29, 2019: https://www.govinfo.gov/app/details/STATUTE-102/STATUTE-102-Pg2853

Public Law 107-296, Homeland Security Act of 2002, November 25, 2002. As of April 29, 2019: https://www.govinfo.gov/app/details/PLAW-107publ296

Public Law 109-295, Department of Homeland Security Appropriations Act, 2007, Title VI, Post-Katrina Emergency Management Reform Act of 2006, October 4, 2006. As of May 5, 2019: https://www.govinfo.gov/app/details/PLAW-109publ295

Public Law 110-69, America Creating Opportunities to Meaningfully Promote Excellence in Technology, Education, and Science (COMPETES) Act, August 9, 2007. As of May 16, 2019: https://www.govinfo.gov/app/details/PLAW-110publ69

Public Law 111-358, America Creating Opportunities to Meaningfully Promote Excellence in Technology, Education, and Science (COMPETES) Reauthorization Act of 2010, January 4, 2011. As of May 16, 2019: https://www.govinfo.gov/app/details/PLAW-111publ358

Public Law 112-29, Leahy–Smith America Invents Act, September 16, 2011. As of May 1, 2019: https://www.govinfo.gov/app/details/PLAW-112publ29

Public Law 114-153, Defend Trade Secrets Act of 2016, May 11, 2016. As of May 1, 2019: https://www.govinfo.gov/app/details/PLAW-114publ153

Public Law 115-278, Cybersecurity and Infrastructure Security Agency Act of 2018, November 16, 2018.

Public Law 115-387, Countering Weapons of Mass Destruction Act of 2018, December 21, 2018.

Qualitex Co. v. Jacobson Prods. Co., 514 U.S. 159 (1995).

Randall, Alice, *The Wind Done Gone*, Boston: Houghton Mifflin, 2001.

Ridge, Tom, Secretary, U.S. Department of Homeland Security, "Delegation to the General Counsel," Delegation 0400.2, September 14, 2004.

Sands, Geneva, "What Isn't Getting Done at the Department of Homeland Security During the Shutdown," CNN, January 15, 2019. As of February 15, 2019: https://www.cnn.com/2019/01/15/politics/homeland-security-dhs-shutdown/index.html

State St. Bank & Trust Co. v. Signature Fin. Grp., 149 F.3d 1368 (Fed. Cir. 1998), *cert. denied*, 525 U.S. 1093 (1999).

SunTrust Bank v. Houghton Mifflin Co., 268 F.3d 1257 (11th Cir. 2001).

Technology Programs Law Division, Office of the General Counsel, U.S. Department of Homeland Security, "Intellectual Property: Enabling Mission Success," April 9, 2018.

Technology Transfer Program, National Aeronautics and Space Administration, homepage, undated. As of May 2, 2019: https://technology.nasa.gov/

TPLD—*See* Technology Programs Law Division.

Transportation Security Administration, *TSA Strategy: 2018–2026*, Washington, D.C., c. 2018a. As of April 29, 2019: https://www.tsa.gov/about/strategy

Transportation Security Administration, *2018 Biennial National Strategy for Transportation Security: Report to Congress*, Washington, D.C.: U.S. Department of Homeland Security, April 4, 2018b. As of April 27, 2019: https://www.tsa.gov/sites/default/files/foia-readingroom/final_2018_nsts_signed.pdf

Truswal Sys. Corp. v. Hydro-Air Eng'g, Inc., 813 F.2d 1207 (Fed. Cir. 1987).

TSA—*See* Transportation Security Administration.

USCG—*See* U.S. Coast Guard.

USCIS—*See* U.S. Citizenship and Immigration Services.

U.S. Citizenship and Immigration Services, "About USCIS," Washington D.C., undated. As of February 13, 2019: https://www.uscis.gov/aboutus

U.S. Citizenship and Immigration Services, "Directorates and Program Offices," Washington, D.C., last updated July 28, 2010. As of February 13, 2019: https://www.uscis.gov/about-us/directorates-and-program-offices

U.S. Citizenship and Immigration Services, "Our History," Washington, D.C., last updated May 25, 2011. As of February 13, 2019: https://www.uscis.gov/about-us/our-history

U.S. Citizenship and Immigration Services, *USCIS Strategic Plan 2017–2021*, Washington, D.C., November 16, 2016. As of April 29, 2019:
https://www.uscis.gov/sites/default/files/USCIS/About%20Us/
Budget%2C%20Planning%20and%20Performance/
USCIS_2017-2021_Strategic_Plan.pdf

U.S. Citizenship and Immigration Services, "What We Do," Washington, D.C., last updated April 12, 2018a. As of February 13, 2019:
https://www.uscis.gov/about-us/what-we-do

U.S. Citizenship and Immigration Services, "A Day in the Life of USCIS," Washington, D.C., last updated April 20, 2018b. As of February 12, 2019:
https://www.uscis.gov/about-us/a-day-life-uscis

U.S. Citizenship and Immigration Services, "USCIS Organizational Chart," Washington, D.C., last updated August 6, 2018c. As of May 4, 2019:
https://www.uscis.gov/about-us/uscis-organizational-chart

U.S. Coast Guard, "United States Coast Guard Organization Chart," undated. As of May 4, 2019:
https://www.uscg.mil/Units/Organization/

U.S. Coast Guard, *U.S. Department of Homeland Security Component Overview: U.S. Coast Guard—2016 Presidential Transition*, Washington, D.C., c. 2016. As of February 15, 2019:
https://www.uscg.mil/Portals/0/documents/
PTT_USCG1.pdf?ver=2016-09-06-163615-050

U.S. Coast Guard, *Coast Guard Strategic Plan 2018–2022*, Washington, D.C., c. 2018. As of April 29, 2019:
https://www.uscg.mil/alwaysready/

U.S. Coast Guard, *United States Coast Guard Posture Statement: 2019 Budget Overview, 2017 Performance Highlights*, Washington, D.C., c. 2019.

U.S. Code, Title 8, Aliens and Nationality; Chapter 12, Immigration and Nationality; Subchapter I, General Provisions; Section 1101, Definitions. As of May 24, 2019:
https://www.govinfo.gov/app/details/USCODE-2011-title8/
USCODE-2011-title8-chap12-subchapI-sec1101

U.S. Code, Title 10, Armed Forces; Subtitle A, General Military Law; Part IV, Service, Supply, and Procurement; Chapter 134, Miscellaneous Administrative Provisions; Subchapter II, Miscellaneous Administrative Authority; Section 2260, Licensing of Intellectual Property: Retention of Fees. As of April 29, 2019:
https://www.govinfo.gov/app/details/USCODE-2017-title10/
USCODE-2017-title10-subtitleA-partIV-chap134-subchapII-sec2260

U.S. Code, Title 10, Armed Forces; Subtitle A, General Military Law; Part IV, Service, Supply, and Procurement; Chapter 137, Procurement Generally; Section 2320, Rights in Technical Data. As of May 1, 2019: https://www.govinfo.gov/app/details/USCODE-2017-title10/ USCODE-2017-title10-subtitleA-partIV-chap137-sec2320

U.S. Code, Title 14, Coast Guard; Part I, Regular Coast Guard; Chapter 17, Administration; Section 638, Coast Guard Ensigns and Pennants. As of May 16, 2019: https://www.govinfo.gov/app/details/USCODE-2012-title14/ USCODE-2012-title14-partI-chap17-sec638

U.S. Code, Title 14, Coast Guard; Part I, Regular Coast Guard; Chapter 17, Administration; Section 639, Penalty for Unauthorized Use of Words "Coast Guard." As of May 4, 2019: https://www.govinfo.gov/app/details/USCODE-2012-title14/ USCODE-2012-title14-partI-chap17-sec639

U.S. Code, Title 15, Commerce and Trade; Chapter 22, Trademarks; Subchapter I, The Principal Register; Section 1051, Application for Registration; Verification. As of May 1, 2019: https://www.govinfo.gov/app/details/USCODE-2017-title15/ USCODE-2017-title15-chap22-subchapI-sec1051

U.S. Code, Title 15, Commerce and Trade; Chapter 22, Trademarks; Subchapter III, General Provisions; Section 1114, Remedies; Infringement; Innocent Infringement by Printers and Publishers. As of May 1, 2019: https://www.govinfo.gov/app/details/USCODE-2017-title15/ USCODE-2017-title15-chap22-subchapIII-sec1114

U.S. Code, Title 15, Commerce and Trade; Chapter 22, Trademarks; Subchapter III, General Provisions; Section 1127, Construction and Definitions; Intent of Chapter. As of May 1, 2019: https://www.govinfo.gov/app/details/USCODE-2017-title15/ USCODE-2017-title15-chap22-subchapIII-sec1127

U.S. Code, Title 17, Copyrights; Chapter 1, Subject Matter and Scope of Copyright; Section 105, Subject Matter of Copyright: United States Government Works. As of May 1, 2019: https://www.govinfo.gov/app/details/USCODE-2010-title17/ USCODE-2010-title17-chap1-sec105

U.S. Code, Title 18, Crimes and Criminal Procedure; Part I, Crimes; Chapter 90, Protection of Trade Secrets; Section 1833, Exceptions to Prohibitions. As of May 1, 2019: https://www.govinfo.gov/app/details/USCODE-2017-title18/ USCODE-2017-title18-partI-chap90-sec1833

U.S. Code, Title 18, Crimes and Criminal Procedure; Part I, Crimes; Chapter 90, Protection of Trade Secrets; Section 1836, Civil Proceedings. As of April 29, 2019:
https://www.govinfo.gov/app/details/USCODE-2017-title18/
USCODE-2017-title18-partI-chap90-sec1836

U.S. Code, Title 28, Judiciary and Judicial Procedure; Part IV, Jurisdiction and Venue; Chapter 91, United States Court of Federal Claims; Section 1498, Patent and Copyright Cases. As of April 29, 2019:
https://www.govinfo.gov/app/details/USCODE-2017-title28/
USCODE-2017-title28-partIV-chap91-sec1498

U.S. Code, Title 35, Patents. As of April 29, 2019:
https://www.govinfo.gov/app/details/USCODE-2017-title35/

U.S. Code, Title 41, Public Contracts; Subtitle I, Federal Procurement Policy; Division A, General; Chapter 1, Definitions; Subchapter I, Subtitle Definitions; Section 116, Technical Data. As of April 29, 2019:
https://www.govinfo.gov/app/details/USCODE-2017-title41/
USCODE-2017-title41-subtitleI-divsnA-chap1-subchapI-sec116

U.S. Customs and Border Protection, *Vision and Strategy 2020: U.S. Customs and Border Protection Strategic Plan*, Washington, D.C., 0215-0315, March 2015. As of February 13, 2019:
https://www.cbp.gov/sites/default/files/documents/CBP-Vision-Strategy-2020.pdf

U.S. Customs and Border Protection, "Laboratories and Scientific Services," Washington, D.C., last modified March 7, 2017a. As of February 13, 2019:
https://www.cbp.gov/about/labs-scientific-svcs

U.S. Customs and Border Protection, "Global Entry," Washington, D.C., last modified October 2, 2017b. As of February 14, 2019:
https://www.cbp.gov/travel/trusted-traveler-programs/global-entry

U.S. Customs and Border Protection, "NEXUS," Washington, D.C., last modified October 2, 2017c. As of February 14, 2019:
https://www.cbp.gov/travel/trusted-traveler-programs/nexus

U.S. Customs and Border Protection, "CBP Organization Chart," last modified October 25, 2017d. As of May 4, 2019:
https://www.cbp.gov/document/publications/cbp-organization-chart

U.S. Customs and Border Protection, "CBP Through the Years," Washington, D.C., last modified November 8, 2017e. As of February 13, 2019:
https://www.cbp.gov/about/history

U.S. Customs and Border Protection, "Missing Migrant Program Expands Life-Saving Efforts Across 4200 Square Miles in the Rio Grande Valley," Washington, D.C., press release, July 18, 2018. As of February 18, 2019:
https://www.cbp.gov/newsroom/local-media-release/
missing-migrant-program-expands-life-saving-efforts-across-4200-square

U.S. Customs and Border Protection, "CTPAT: Customs Trade Partnership Against Terrorism," last modified March 26, 2019a. As of April 27, 2019:
https://www.cbp.gov/border-security/ports-entry/cargo-security/ctpat

U.S. Customs and Border Protection, "About CBP," Washington, D.C., April 18, 2019b. As of February 13, 2019:
https://www.cbp.gov/about

U.S. Department of Homeland Security, "About CISA," Washington, D.C., undated. As of February 13, 2019:
https://www.dhs.gov/cisa/about-cisa

U.S. Department of Homeland Security, *Quadrennial Homeland Security Review Report: A Strategic Framework for a Secure Homeland*, Washington, D.C., February 2010. As of April 29, 2019:
https://www.dhs.gov/publication/2010-quadrennial-homeland-security-review-qhsr

U.S. Department of Homeland Security, "U.S. Immigration and Customs Enforcement," June 7, 2011. As of May 5, 2019:
https://www.dhs.gov/xlibrary/assets/org-chart-ice.pdf

U.S. Department of Homeland Security, *National Infrastructure Protection Plan 2013: Partnering for Critical Infrastructure Security and Reliance*, Washington, D.C., c. 2013. As of April 27, 2019:
https://www.dhs.gov/publication/
nipp-2013-partnering-critical-infrastructure-security-and-resilience

U.S. Department of Homeland Security, "Ensure Resilience to Disasters," Washington, D.C., last published March 21, 2016a. As of April 29, 2019:
https://www.dhs.gov/building-resilient-nation

U.S. Department of Homeland Security, "Secure and Manage Our Borders," Washington, D.C., last published March 21, 2016b. As of April 29, 2019:
https://www.dhs.gov/secure-and-manage-borders

U.S. Department of Homeland Security, "Prevent Terrorism and Enhance Security," Washington, D.C., last published May 6, 2016c. As of April 29, 2019:
https://www.dhs.gov/prevent-terrorism-and-enhance-security

U.S. Department of Homeland Security, "Mature and Strengthen the Homeland Security Enterprise," Washington, D.C., last published October 24, 2016d. As of April 29, 2019:
https://www.dhs.gov/strengthen-security-enterprise

U.S. Department of Homeland Security, "Secretary Nielsen Announces the Establishment of the Countering Weapons of Mass Destruction Office," press release, December 7, 2017. As of February 13, 2019:
https://www.dhs.gov/news/2017/12/07/secretary-nielsen-announces-establishment-countering-weapons-mass-destruction-office

U.S. Department of Homeland Security, *Department of Homeland Security U.S. Immigration and Customs Enforcement, Budget Overview: Fiscal Year 2018 Congressional Justification*, Washington, D.C., c. 2018a. As of February 17, 2019:
https://www.dhs.gov/sites/default/files/publications/ICE%20FY18%20Budget.pdf

U.S. Department of Homeland Security, "NPPD at a Glance," Washington, D.C., February 23, 2018b. As of February 13, 2019:
https://www.dhs.gov/sites/default/files/publications/
nppd-at-a-glance-bifold-02132018-508.pdf

U.S. Department of Homeland Security, "Safeguard and Secure Cyberspace," Washington, D.C., last published May 17, 2018c. As of April 29, 2019:
https://www.dhs.gov/safeguard-and-secure-cyberspace

U.S. Department of Homeland Security, "Enforce and Administer Our Immigration Laws," Washington, D.C., last published August 15, 2018d. As of April 29, 2019:
https://www.dhs.gov/administer-immigration-laws

U.S. Department of Homeland Security, "Countering Weapons of Mass Destruction Office," Washington, D.C., last published December 21, 2018e. As of February 13, 2019:
https://www.dhs.gov/countering-weapons-mass-destruction-office

U.S. Government Accountability Office, *Federal Emergency Management Agency: Additional Planning and Data Collection Could Help Improve Workforce Management Efforts*, Washington, D.C., GAO-15-437, July 9, 2015. As of April 29, 2019:
https://www.gao.gov/products/GAO-15-437

U.S. Government Accountability Office, *2017 Hurricanes and Wildfires: Initial Observations on the Federal Response and Key Recovery Challenges*, Washington, D.C., GAO-18-472, September 4, 2018. As of April 29, 2019:
https://www.gao.gov/products/GAO-18-472

U.S. Immigration and Customs Enforcement, "HSI Forensic Laboratory," Washington, D.C., last updated January 3, 2018a. As of February 13, 2019:
https://www.ice.gov/hsi-fl

U.S. Immigration and Customs Enforcement, "Intellectual Property Rights," Washington, D.C., last updated March 12, 2018b. As of February 15, 2019:
https://www.ice.gov/iprcenter

U.S. Immigration and Customs Enforcement, "What We Do," Washington, D.C., last updated December 4, 2018c. As of February 14, 2019:
https://www.ice.gov/overview

U.S. Immigration and Customs Enforcement, "Who We Are," Washington, D.C., last updated December 14, 2018d. As of February 14, 2019:
https://www.ice.gov/about

U.S. Immigration and Customs Enforcement, "Celebrating the History of ICE," Washington, D.C., last updated March 1, 2019. As of February 13, 2019: https://www.ice.gov/features/history

U.S. Patent and Trademark Office, "Examining of Secrecy Order Cases," *Manual of Patent Examining Procedure*, Chapter 0100, "Secrecy, Access, National Security, and Foreign Filing," Section 130, R-11.2013, 2013. As of February 13, 2019: https://www.uspto.gov/web/offices/pac/mpep/s130.html

U.S. Patent and Trademark Office, "General Information Concerning Patents," Alexandria, Va., October 2015. As of February 13, 2019: https://www.uspto.gov/patents-getting-started/ general-information-concerning-patents

USPTO—*See* U.S. Patent and Trademark Office.

U.S. Senate, "Providing for the Registration and Protection of Trade-Marks Used in Commerce to Carry Out the Provisions of Certain International Conventions May 14," Washington, D.C., Senate Report 1333, 79th Congress, 2nd Session, March 5, 1946.

U.S. Statutes at Large, Vol. 1, First Congress, 2nd Session, Chapter VII, an act to promote the progress of useful arts, April 10, 1790.

Warner-Jenkinson Co. v. Hilton Davis Chem. Co., 520 U.S. 17 (1997).

World Intellectual Property Organization, "Innovation and Intellectual Property," undated. As of February 13, 2019: https://www.wipo.int/ip-outreach/en/ipday/2017/ innovation_and_intellectual_property.html